The Crow Flies
Backwards
and Other New
Zen Koans

"This book opens with perhaps the best written
introduction to koan work I've encountered.
With warmth and humor leavening his erudition,
Bolleter strips away unnecessary mystique and
preserves the delights of their mystery and the
seriousness of their play, enlivening lay practice
and anchoring koans in our everyday experience."

—Robert Rosenbaum, author of *Walking the Way*

"Touching and insightful—filled with intimacy and
deep humanity. Ross Bolleter reveals working with
Zen koans as a creative and liberating practice."

—Rafe Martin, author of *Before Buddha Was Buddha*

"A beautiful, fun, and at the very
same time profoundly challenging book.
You want to know what wisdom looks like?
You can't do much better than this book."

—James Ishmael Ford, author of
Introduction to Zen Koans

The Crow Flies Backwards and Other New Zen Koans

ROSS BOLLETER

Wisdom

Wisdom Publications
199 Elm Street
Somerville, MA 02144 USA
wisdompubs.org

Library of Congress Cataloging-in-Publication Data
Names: Bolleter, Ross, editor.
Title: The crow flies backwards and other new zen koans / Ross Bolleter.
Description: Somerville, MA: Wisdom Publications, 2018. | Includes bibli-
    ographical references. |
Identifiers: LCCN 2017048413 (print) | LCCN 2017050857 (ebook) | ISBN
    9781614293132 (ebook) | ISBN 9781614292944 (paperback)
Subjects: LCSH: Koan. | BISAC: RELIGION / Buddhism / Zen (see also
    PHILOSOPHY / Zen). | RELIGION / Buddhism / Sacred Writings. |
    RELIGION / Buddhism / Rituals & Practice.
Classification: LCC BQ9289.5 (ebook) | LCC BQ9289.5 .C76 2018 (print) |
    DDC 294.3/443—dc23
LC record available at https://lccn.loc.gov/2017048413

ISBN 978-1-61429-294-4   ebook ISBN 978-1-61429-313-2
22 21 20 19 18   5 4 3 2 1

Cover design by Phil Pascuzzo. Interior design by Gopa & Ted2, Inc.
Set in Sabon LT Pro 10.25/14.7. Photo of Ross Bolleter by Antoinette
Carrier, Bedford, Western Australia, 2013.

Wisdom Publications' books are printed on acid-free paper and meet the
guidelines for permanence and durability of the Production Guidelines for
Book Longevity of the Council on Library Resources.

♻ This book was produced with environmental
mindfulness. For more information, please visit
wisdompubs.org/wisdom-environment.

Printed in the United States of America.   Please visit fscus.org.

For Rose and Charlotte,
my grandchildren

Contents

Preface

The Crow Flies Backwards is a collection of 108 Western koans, together with my commentaries on 40 of them. These commentaries provide guidance as to how to engage with a particular koan, as well as its sources. In the opening chapters, I address the nature of the koan, what it means to sit with a koan, and how koans work on our heart-mind and in our lives. Finally, I have interspersed my commentaries with various "investigations" especially concerning the nature of time. Most of these investigations have koan content.

Koans resist precise definition; however, we can say broadly that a koan is a formulation—sometimes couched as a fundamental question, such as "Who am I?"—that Zen practitioners inquire into in order to awaken to their true nature. By "true nature" I mean our nature beneath and beyond such notions as a socially constructed self, personality, or "an inner ghostly self" that manipulates the senses and to which we accord ownership of our thoughts and dreams.

After an initial awakening to our true nature, further koans are employed to enable us to more fully embody our awakening and over time to express, to mature, and ultimately to assimilate it so thoroughly that we forget it in the act of living it. This book also includes Western koans that reflect these later stages of the koan path.

By "Western koans" I mean, broadly, koans deriving from Australian, American, European, and South American sources. Regarding the koans from Australia, my native land, I have chosen several that have as their source the indigenous peoples of Australia.

The Crow Flies Backwards is intended for students and teachers of the Zen Way, and indeed everyone and anyone interested in Zen, especially in its Western unfolding. This book can be used to supplement the traditional koan literature as it comes down to us through Chinese and Japanese sources—or it can be used as a stand-alone investigation.

I have developed some of the koans included here from dialogues with my Dharma successors and students, some of whom have also created koans included below. Others have found the koans in this book efficacious for investigation, so we have begun the process of "road testing" them.

In writing this book, I have given prominence to koans drawn from lay life, especially koans that have as their themes sexuality and childbirth, relationships, work, and money: themes that are almost entirely absent from the monastic koan traditions that come down to us from China and Japan. I have also included a variety of koans that focus on time. This latter theme is of course not absent from Chinese and Japanese koan traditions, but given our Western culture's obsession with time and its anxieties about it, I felt it important to give it prominence.

Although *The Crow Flies Backwards* focuses on Western koans, I am not suggesting for a moment that we should abandon the powerful and efficacious Chinese and Japanese koan traditions we have inherited. Rather we should feel free to *extend* those traditions by creating a koan literature that reflects our contemporary lives and culture. It is my hope that the koans and commentaries in *The Crow Flies Backwards* will encourage this undertaking.

More than thirty-five years ago, at the outset of my first sesshin, Robert Aitken gave me the koan of Zhaozhou's "Mu," and over the next several years I worked through the early stages of the koan curriculum with him. I continued my journey on the koan path with John Tarrant as my teacher, completing koan study with him in the early 1990s. I am deeply grateful to Robert Aitken and to John Tarrant for their guidance and inspiration over those many years. In terms of the Zen Way, my ruling passion was koan work, and they were there to support me at every turn.

I got my first taste of what a Western koan might be working with John Tarrant, who would improvise koans on the spot for the happiness of all beings. I enjoyed the challenge and the playfulness of John's approach, and have continued it with my own successors and students. *The Crow Flies Backwards* is the upshot.

My gratitude to:

Susan Murphy: Back in 1999, Susan gave me a booklet of koans titled *Bright Darkness: 53 Koans*—some selected, some created by her—for my birthday. One of the koans in her collection was "Crows fly backwards," which gave me the title koan for this book. Several other koans from her collection are also in this book. I am grateful to Susan for her constant love, encouragement, and support over the many years.

Mari Rhydwen: Mari is my co-teacher in the Zen Group of Western Australia, and I am grateful to her for her teaching and for her inspiration, support, and encouragement over the longest time, as well as for allowing me to include, along with other contributions, her inspiring Three Girls Dream in this book.

Arthur Wells: for generously allowing me to include several of the koans from the collection that he is creating, titled *Koans to Embody*, as well as making valuable contributions and suggestions. And for his encouragement and support over many years, including his encouragement of this book.

Glenn Wallis: for providing several fine koans for this book, and making valuable suggestions. And for his encouragement and support over the many years, including his encouragement of this enterprise.

Bob Joyner: for allowing me to include his cogent account of practice and realization in this book, and for his support and encouragement over the many years.

Kathy Shiels: who proofread *The Crow Flies Backwards* in an earlier manifestation and offered many valuable suggestions. And for her warm encouragement of the book in all its stages, as well as for her fine contributions to it.

Phillip McNamara: for generously allowing me to include his essay "Working with 'Who Is Hearing That Sound?'" and for his rich offering of koans to the Crow.

Michael Wright: for his guidance and assistance in matters of Nyoongar culture and spirituality in the title chapter, and his warm encouragement of the Crow.

The many other members of the Zen Group of Western Australia who contributed koans and stories to *The Crow Flies Backwards*, making it a celebration of our sangha in all its variety and liveliness.

The Council of the Zen Group of Western Australia: for affording me a sabbatical from teaching so that I could work on this book and for their support and care over the many years.

Bob Gray: for his support for the Crow, and for his warm encouragement for me to write it.

Tony Coote of the Sydney Zen Centre: for his contribution of the story "Save me, Bill."

Chris Barker and Jane Taylor of the Castlemaine Zen Group: for their contributions to Crow mind.

Amanda Bolleter, my daughter: for her love, support, and encouragement, always.

Julian Bolleter, my son: for reading an early draft of this book and making invaluable suggestions as well as providing me with important material, and for his love, support, and encouragement, always.

Antoinette Carrier, my partner: for her enduring support and encouragement over the many years, and for her constant love that inspires my work and makes it possible.

Dr. Jan Resnick: who read an earlier version of the Crow and made important suggestions, as well as encouraging this enterprise.

Josh Bartok, executive editor at Wisdom Publications: for his fine editing of the manuscript and his invaluable support for the project of writing a book of commentaries on Western koans.

Ashley Benning: for her fine copyediting on the manuscript.

Ben Gleason, production editor at Wisdom: for his assistance with the permissions and his help and guidance in bringing the Crow home through its several stages.

Possum, my cat and constant companion in writing and composing, happy to delete a stray paragraph as she parades over the computer keyboard.

An extract from the introduction to this book can be found heading a forum involving Joan Sutherland, Bodhin Kjolhede, and Judy Roitman on the theme of "Koans: How We Work with Them and How They Work on Us," in *Buddhadharma: The Practitioner's Quarterly*, Summer 2015: 54–63. My thanks to Koun Franz, editor of *Buddhadharma*, for encouraging me to be involved in that project, which was seminal for this one.

PART I
Prelude

Introduction: The Nature of the Koan and How Koans Came to the West

IN A CERTAIN SENSE, koans—like poems or jokes—can't be defined precisely. However, we can say broadly that a koan is a formulation that, when deeply explored in meditation, provides us with a means to awaken to who we truly are, as well as to express, deepen, and embody that awakening in our lives. Koans are protean; they can appear, for instance, as a verse, a folk story, a teacher's words, or a dialogue between teacher and student. Here is a traditional koan in verse from unknown sources that intimates the mystery of the Way:

> From a well that has never been dug,
> water ripples in a spring that does not flow;
> someone with no shadow or form is drawing
>   the water.

Sometimes people encounter the Way in times of crisis, such as the death of a loved one or a life-threatening illness or through intense physical and emotional suffering. On such occasions, deep questions may surface: "Why do I suffer?" "Who am I without my loved one?" "Who am I in the face of my own mortality?" "What purpose does my life have?" Any such fundamental questions can be taken up as a koan—and our anguish spurs and gives us the tenacity to stay with the koan until it resolves.

It needs to be said at the outset that *koan* is not a mere synonym for "dilemma." And yet when we sit in meditation with certain dilemmas of our lives, we can wear out the intellect in the cat's cradle of opposing considerations and end by sitting with just our not knowing. If we can endure there, continuing our questioning, clarifications may arise unexpectedly out of nowhere.

Apart from koans that may arise from harrowing experiences and dilemmas, it is good to discover—as well as to create—koans from within the weave of our lives. For me, the following is such a koan, rich in possibilities concerning time and creative engagement with life, as well as the mystery of words:

> When he was in his eighties, my father was knocked down by a delivery van. In hospital they put him in "treatment," prior to admitting him as a patient. Although no one could find time to get him a bottle to piss in, four staff members came round with their clipboards during the three hours he waited there, to ask him his age. He generously gave each of them a fresh response—"twenty-one," "ninety-eight," "forty-seven," and finally, "two hundred!"

Extending Chinese and Japanese Koan Traditions in the West

By advocating that we work with Western koans, I am in no way suggesting that we abandon the noble koan traditions that come down to us primarily from the Chan schools of China and the Zen schools of Japan. Such a legacy is a matter of wonder and is a tremendously efficacious tool for awakening and for integrating our awakening into our lives

So, rather than abandoning tradition, let us feel free to extend it. There are good reasons for this: the koan literature that we inherit comes to us almost entirely from patriarchal monastic traditions so that there are, understandably, lacunae especially regarding relationships, family, love, sex, childbirth, child rearing, work, and money. As lay Zen practitioners, we have an opportunity, even a responsibility, to develop koans that reflect these themes.

In *The Crow Flies Backwards* I also derive and create Western koans that focus on time and timelessness, along with the closely related theme of memory. These themes aren't absent in Chinese and Japanese koan traditions, but they too can be extended.

Consider the opening of Kenneth Slessor's great poem "Five Bells":

Time that is moved by little fidget wheels
Is not my time, the flood that does not flow.
Between the double and the single bell
Of a ship's hour, between a round of bells
From the dark warship riding there below,
I have lived many lives, and this one life
Of Joe, long dead, who lives between five bells.

Another koan with the theme of time and timelessness is William Blake's "Eternity is in love with the productions of time" from his *Marriage of Heaven and Hell*. Both of these koans are explored later on.

Unlike the koans from our Zen monastic inheritance, koans from Western sources have no formal traditional responses, so both teacher and student must discover their own. This is an opportunity to be creative and to play. As a Zen teacher who is also an improvising musician and composer, I find joy in working with my students in this way, as well as creating koans in dialogue with them:

> "Still wandering in your mind?" I asked a student.
> "You bet."
> "What's there?"
> "Oh, gray sky, the sun on the salmon gums."

How Koans Came West

The use of the koan as a teaching tool entered the West through the efforts of pioneering teachers such as Soyen Shaku (1860–1919), who taught Ida and Alexander Russell and their family at their home outside of San Francisco in 1905. (According to scholar Rick Fields, it seems that Ida Russell was the first person in the United States to undertake koan study.) Soyen Shaku's student Nyogen Senzaki (1876–1958) was the first major Zen teacher to reside in the United States. He compiled his *101 Zen Stories* in 1919 (the book saw a later iteration as *Zen Flesh, Zen Bones*) and used koans in his teaching in San Francisco at least from the 1920s onwards. Sokei-an Shigetsu Sasaki (1882–1945) was a Rinzai master who pioneered the Zen Way in New York in the 1930s. Sokei-an employed koans with his students, including Ruth Fuller Everett (1892–1967) who became his wife. As Ruth Fuller Sasaki, she made an inestimable contribution to the development of Zen in the West through her translations of such major Zen texts as *The Record of Lin-chi, The Recorded Sayings of Layman P'ang,* and *Zen Dust: The History of the Koan and Koan Study in Rinzai (Lin-chi) Zen.*

As noted above, koans that come down to us from Chinese sources may take a variety of forms—a verse, a teacher's words, a dialogue between teacher and student, and so on. Similarly, for Western koans we will draw on verses, dialogues between teachers and students, lines from the Bible, literature both ancient and modern, and personal stories. There are also koans to be discovered within the weave of our lives, as well as in our contemporary culture. I explore these territories and encourage my students to do likewise.

I have endeavored to find or create Western koans that are appropriate for the student at various stages of the training path: for instance, the initial koans of emptiness which provide a vehicle for the student to awaken to their true and timeless nature; after that, koans which encourage the student to experience a return to the differentiated realm of color and form after their awakening experience. There are also koans that help the student to embody their awakening in the many and varied circumstances of their life, and others that elicit an awakening to the mystery of words. Finally, there are koans that assist the student to mature their awakening and ultimately assimilate it—and forget it—completely.

In terms of our deepest nature, we live at the intersection of sameness and difference. Indeed, we are that very intersection: vast yet utterly individual, with not a hairsbreadth between. It is my hope that *The Crow Flies Backwards* will provide a means to experience that matter and take it into our lives. Who, after all, is living this life?

What Does It Mean to Sit with a Koan? 1

KOANS WIDELY EMPLOYED to help us awaken to our true nature include Zhaozhou's "Mu," Bassui Zenji's "Who is hearing that sound?" "Who am I?" and "What is it?" In this chapter I will employ the koan "Who am I?" as an exemplar and guide to working with your initial koan. I have chosen to do this because, regardless of our gender, our cultural background, or our life circumstances, we are all familiar with "Who am I?" as a fundamental question. It might be assumed that such familiarity runs the risk of entrapping the student in thoughts concerning a socially and personally constructed self and customary roles. However, the experience of students working on the koan "Who am I?" is that, in short order, it brings them face to face with the mystery that lies deeper than such matters.

Working with the Koan "Who Am I?"

In all the varying circumstances of your life, ask yourself and continue to ask yourself, "Who am I?"

Let your curiosity regarding this matter be boundless.

It is vital to engage with the koan "Who am I?" through regular daily seated meditation, through *zazen*. It's also good to walk it into your life. Even the busiest days provide opportunities to return to the koan: while your computer is booting up, before answering your phone, or as you are walking between tasks. Robert Aitken called these opportunities "islands of practice." Apart from their efficacy in terms of working with "Who am I?" these brief homecomings can be deeply refreshing and subtly shift the energy in difficult situations.

Great Faith, Great Doubt, and Great Determination

The qualities traditionally deemed necessary to awaken are great faith, great doubt, and great determination. The cross-legged posture of zazen is the perfect expression of this tripod, for your left knee on the mat, your backside on the cushion, and your right knee on the other side of the mat represent great faith, great doubt, and great determination without remainder!

Really, great faith means trusting that we are intrinsically awake and have been so from the beginning, while in the same breath striving to awaken for the first, dearest, freshest time. Koun Yamada (1907–1989) expressed it this way:

> This great root of faith is not just a tepid faith. It is a thoroughgoing belief that will settle for nothing less than complete awakening, and is rooted firmly in the ground like a huge tree, immovable in the face of even the strongest gale.

Yamada also said, "I want to be a great tree shading all beings." By this he meant that his realization, and his teaching that flowed from it, were not just for himself, but for the benefit of all beings, both sentient and nonsentient. This is the bodhisattva path where you enlighten yourself and others in the midst of the passions, in the midst of the suffering world. *Bodhisattva* means "enlightened being," a being who is becoming enlightened and a being who enlightens others. Yamada was Robert Aitken's principal teacher, and Aitken Roshi in turn was my first teacher. I am grateful for that great tree sheltering all beings that has made my own path possible.

The expression "great doubt" is puzzling for many people coming to Zen. In general, religions and spiritual paths don't readily accept doubt, let alone encourage it, most especially concerning their own tenets. Great doubt surely includes the matter of accepting our own doubts: for instance our doubt as to whether we can come to awakening at all or whether, given the brevity of our life, we have time enough to come to awakening. Faced with such doubts, we include them, saying: "I am going ahead with my doubts."

Doubt may also be associated with the withering away of our delusions and attachments. I remember a student who was working on the koan "Mu" telling me that his dreams were full of forests being destroyed and tumbling silently into the void. He would awaken terrified. I actually felt that what was happening for him was most promising and encouraged him to continue.

Doubt can also be associated with views such as: "I

don't deserve to awaken when there is so much suffering in the world." To this I respond: "But your awakening is your birthright. You don't have to deserve it any more than you have to deserve your life."

Doubt fuels the Way. The deeper we go, the more our cherished ideas are brought into question. Notions like our identity and its substantiality, for example, begin to be less and less pressing.

In *sesshin*, the intensive meditation retreats of the Zen tradition, we get to test this. After a couple of days the notion of myself as a musician fades away at the edges of the moment. After sesshin, the musician role feels light, insubstantial, almost strange to take up again, and yet I do, in the spirit of play.

Deeper in, the soft avalanche of ideas that we once held dear continues. We reach a place where we've run out of ideas and are blocked: we really don't know who we are. Whatever doubts arise about the validity or sensibleness of the enterprise at that time, we just plough them under and continue to ask, "Who am I?" regardless. It doesn't make any sense to persist like this, we just do. Slowly we unite with the koan, and it with us: we become intimate. Like this, great doubt is becoming intimate with your koan.

The expression "great determination" means that we commit to awaken to who we truly are, regardless of difficulties and impediments. To this end, we bring the koan "Who am I?" into our life: sitting it, walking it, sleeping it. We keep returning to that koan, even though it makes no sense to return. We return regardless.

Realizing the Way is not simply a solo effort though. The Way beckons; the Way calls. What is the calling of the Way? Listen. Listen.

We try to break through to the Way, even as it receives us, and even indeed as *it is us*—as it always has been.

What Does It Mean to Resolve a Koan?

People often ask: "Is there a right answer to this koan? Did I get the right answer?" But "right answers" are not the point. If a koan is a question at all, it is a question without an answer. In an important way, there are no *answers* to genuine koans. However, this does not mean that a genuine koan does not have a *resolution*.

At the outset of koan work, the resolution of the koan is the experience of insight into your true nature. This is called *kensho,* or sometimes *satori*. Such an experience feels both ancient and as fresh as this moment. It confirms what has always been *thus*. While awakening is personal, it is recognizable in measure to someone who has had a corresponding experience. When a student comes to me with a genuine experience, it feels as if we are sitting together among the grasses and flowers of the same meadow. There is a sense of ease and inevitability, of being at home together.

The experience of awakening is akin to our "wedding" to the Way, while the long journey of working with subsequent koans corresponds to our marriage to it, which is to say, the unfolding of the Way as our lives. Deepening enlightenment serves to confirm an experience of awakening while widening its aperture. Subsequent koans are employed to move the student on from an awakening experience to prevent them from clinging to emptiness, a grasping which left unchecked poisons practice, as well as life.

Strategies for Working with the Koan "Who Am I?"

It may be helpful to shorten the question "Who am I?" to "Who?" It may likewise be helpful to cue "Who?" to your breath. Cuing the koan, or an abridged form of it, to your breath helps to disperse thoughts and thinking and enables you to settle more readily into the koan, while persistently asking the question raises your enquiring spirit, which is absolutely vital for your journey with the koan. You focus your enquiring spirit on the question as to who you truly are, just as a magnifying glass focuses the rays of the sun to create heat and, finally, fire.

The activity of the mind, especially our self-preoccupied thinking, makes up what the old master Wumen Huikai (1183–1260) called "the mind road." We are all familiar with the mind road with its incessant traffic of planning, remembering, recreating the past, and obsessing about future events—which mostly don't even eventuate! When we work with the koan "Who am I?" we don't get into hand-to-hand combat with thinking; rather we cut off the trails of our thinking by breathing "Who?" and asking "Who am I?" And we continue to do this regardless. It is helpful not to get into blaming yourself when you lose track of the koan. As soon as you realize you are lost, you are home; then you seamlessly renew your questioning by asking: "Who am I?" or breathing "Who?" In this way you practice like rain falls or light moves across a wall over the course of a day.

You continue to deepen your questioning tirelessly to the extreme, regardless of whether you feel deep or shallow, confused or clear. You don't need a pure deep place within in which to practice and awaken, and indeed awakening may occur when you are confused or overwhelmed by emotion—and certainly when you are least expecting it.

How Koans Work on the Heart-Mind and in Our Lives   2

HEART-MIND (*xin* Chinese; *shin* or *kokoro*, Japanese) has three basic meanings: the heart and its functions; mind and its functions; and center or essence. It is the last function of heart-mind—the encounter with our essential nature and the deepening and maturing of that experience—that koans primarily address. However, that is surely not exclusively the case. When we work with koans, we may detect profound changes in feeling, outlook, and engagement with the world, relating to all three meanings of "heart-mind."

The way a koan acts on the heart-mind is mysterious, and if we work with koans in depth—if we engage intimately with them—then our life is changed in ways that have nothing to do with our wishing or willing. We are changed inwardly, as well as in our interactions with others and with the world at large. We find that we come from a different place, and though we look inwards to see what it is, it cannot be viewed. The deep source of our activity is out of reach of our perception and our conceptualizing mind. As Yu Daopo, the donut maker who lived in old China, said of her own awakening to the Way: "For ten thousand years the flowing spring does not know its source."

The Dream, the Koan, and Synchronicity

Regarding the influence of koans on our heart-mind and in our lives, early in my Zen teaching career, I asked several of my students about the effects of koan study on their lives. I was especially interested in the relationship between particular koans that they were working on and how the themes of those koans might play out for them in their interactions with the world, or in their dreams. What I had in mind was Jung's notion of synchronicity as the meaningful coincidence of similar or identical thoughts, dreams, or other events occurring at the same time in different places.

Dr. Mari Rhydwen's response was her account of a dream that she had when working on the koan "Snow in a silver bowl," that she called the Three Girls Dream. The reader is referred to Mari's beautiful retelling of her dream and its relation to the koan in the appendix. At the conclusion of her account, Mari writes:

> Returning to the koan of snow in a silver bowl, via other sisters and more snow, I was able to delight in the way that working with koans is part of a vast dance. It dances itself in dreams and in telephone calls just as much as in the *dokusan* room. I am reminded of Wumen's Caution, "To treat each thought as realization is to trifle with your spirit." There is danger here. Yet, like discovering that the ubiquitous parking spaces that come with years of zazen are a shared secret, there is a sense of sangha involved when the dance I thought I

was dancing alone in the universe turns out to be choreographed to link an infinite cast across the boundary of dream and distance.

Mari gathers us all into that dance and shows us heart-mind, unbounded and limitlessly inclusive. I am grateful to her.

Although the koan of "Snow in a silver bowl" comes from our Chinese Chan heritage, our exploration of this koan in relation to dream tends to give it a Western home, especially as our explorations owe a debt to Carl Jung, who coined the term *synchronicity* and posited its connections to dreams. At the same time, towering in the background of any account of synchronicity is the I Ching, rooted in ancient Chinese traditions and based in a universe of acausal connection evoking intimacy across time and space on a scale that is fathomless beyond reckoning. As an afterthought, we might note the significance of the fact that Jung himself helped to introduce the I Ching to the West.

A Koan on the Theme of Synchronicity

When synchronicities occur, the web of interconnections lights up as emptiness allows. Synchronicities are like sparks from a great conflagration intimating the play of reality beneath and beyond our ordinary causal dualistic thinking.

What is that conflagration?

The Long-Term Effects of Sitting with the Same Koan

Some of my students have been sitting with their first koan for some twenty-five years. Although this may sound frustrating—and of course there is frustration—the changes to their lives over that time have been so marked and so much for the better: a thriving relationship after many earlier failed ones, academic success after very hard beginnings in life, and excellent parenthood after difficult childhood just to name a few. In several instances, although they have had awakening experiences, they have plowed them under and kept going with the same koan. In Korean Zen, practitioners customarily stay with the same koan for life, and I feel that this mode of koan work has much to recommend it.

The long-term effects of koan study on our lives include increasing intimacy with our circumstances: we find we can stay present in situations where we might have previously moved off out of fear. I am thinking of occasions where we must face up to criticism and be present and open to the fear and the shame that we feel. We can also be more readily there for others, even listening ourselves away as they tell their story or express their distress. In this manner, compassion is there for the asking.

Finally, we become more intimate with the world, which no longer feels like some painted backdrop to our fantasies of power and control. Rather, we breathe the world, sleep the world, walk the world, and finally die the world. Moreover, our life feels as though it has been let out at the seams; it feels edgeless and unbounded.

Genuine Awakening and Release from Suffering

The effects of genuine awakening are incalculable. As I write in *Dongshan's Five Ranks: Keys to Enlightenment*:

> We can't know in advance how we will awaken, any more than we can know how we will die. Each of us will die; not all of us will realize. Even if we do realize, it may not be as it is extravagantly described in books like *The Three Pillars of Zen*. Realization may arrive more like the dawn sun lighting a dark hill: picking out first a rock, then a tree, until, after much devoted practice, the entire slope is illuminated.
>
> Or your realization may be sudden, unexpected, and revealing a reality that you never dreamed of, let alone glimpsed before. After the shock and joy come confidence and equanimity in their time. Something has opened that is alive and at ease. Its power and energy surface from unknowable depths, animating our action in the world. We are enlivened, and move others. We preach vigorously with our simple "Good morning," and with our laughter, quickened by wind and sunshine. Our simplest acts—picking up a cup, listening attentively—touch and enliven others.

Bob Joyner, to whom I also addressed my question about the influence of koan work on his life, gives us a picture of how he was living his realization when he was a resident in Perth and doing koan work with me in the mid-90s. Here is an excerpt from his account, which can be found in the appendix:

> Today, with still a way to go, I find myself integrating with much of what goes on around me. I love to travel on public transport, which provides glimpses of so many facets of my human nature. As trees and bushes in the garden, I shimmer in the wind. At the zendo and going to the deli I flow as traffic down the Great Eastern Highway. I live with a general acceptance of people and circumstance without judging. This doesn't happen perfectly or continuously or ideally—and may never—but that is why I continue with daily zazen and endeavor to push along with koan work as best I can. I guess that will always be the case.

With realization, the world walks through our heart, as our heart, and we experience freedom from the mean-spirited, self-centered thinking and activity that close us down and make us unavailable to others. With realization, in measure, we find release from suffering, from the pain and distress resulting from our deluded views about the nature of our self and our relation to the world. Moreover, our suffering is carried differently, if we can speak of it being carried at all. Finally, we may be less afraid of our own dying and more concerned about the death of those we love.

Withal, we get to experience liberation, and compassion and empathy for suffering beings are there for the asking. When it's like this, we can say with Shakespeare's Juliet:

My bounty is as boundless as the sea,
My love as deep; the more I give to thee,
The more I have, for both are infinite.

PART II

Commentaries on Western Koans

Who Am I? 3

THE QUESTION "Who am I?" is deeply embedded in our Western spiritual and philosophical traditions, inviting us to explore the mystery of who we truly are. We know all about who we are in terms of our names and roles; we know who we are in terms of our place in a family and the roles conferred on us by society. For instance, I am the father of Amanda and Julian and the partner of Antoinette; I am a working composer and musician, and, like my peers everywhere, I can reel off various autobiographical details about those matters. However, the question as to *who I am—in depth*—addresses something more, and to experience who we truly are is to open up our life immeasurably and discover that we are not bounded by our skin or our skull; still less are we bounded by our ideas about ourselves.

The question as to who we are in socially constructed terms is important for our formation as individuals, especially in adolescence, where that question is often entangled with others concerning the purpose of our life and how we will invest our life in work and relationship.

When I was at university, I vividly remember my shock on reading the injunction "Know thyself" carved into the limestone portal of the Arts Building. "How can I do that?" I wondered. I'm sure that the incapacity I felt in that moment helped lead me to Zen.

Questions as to who we are may recur throughout our lives, especially in times of crisis. But people don't come to the Way only through crisis; curiosity—or rather passionate curiosity—can be more than enough.

The question of *who* or *what* we truly are can be obscured by our stories arising from past suffering, present confusion, and fears for the future. Yet, when we take up the koan "Who am I?" we persevere, regardless, in the midst of our doubts and demons. Although we may feel we are close to what we take to be our "self"—in fact, not other than it—we may be deluded as to its nature. This is especially the case if we imagine the self to be a kind of "ghost in the machine," an indwelling entity that "owns" and manipulates our hearing, seeing, and understanding.

Descartes wrote: "I think, therefore I am." For Descartes, this formulation—a koan in its own right—couldn't reasonably be doubted, and as a certain certainty, it served as a springboard for his philosophical investigations. There's no smoke without fire. If there are thoughts, surely there must be someone to think them. But how about when you're not thinking? Do you thereby cease to exist? And how about when you are asleep?

Pablo Neruda writes in his poem "Demasiados Nombres" (Too Many Names):

When I sleep every night
What am I called or not called?

And when I awake who am I
if I was not I while I slept?

Sleep plunges us beneath thought and thinking. A snore opens chasms deeper than our names and roles. So who is it who stirs in the jangle of the alarm? Thinking, thinking, thinking—thought after thought arises in mind. Surely there must be someone who thinks them. If there isn't anyone, isn't that intolerable? Isn't that, fundamentally, a very bad joke?

As with our thoughts, so too with our sensations, feelings, and dreams; we assign each of these to this "I" that we take to be the owner and controller of our mental life. Interestingly, from earliest childhood we erect a barrier to protect this controlling imaginary "I," which turns out, not surprisingly, to be particularly vulnerable. As Zen teacher Mari Rhydwen puts it: "We spend a lot of time protecting the me that isn't there."

When we come to awakening, we recognize that this indwelling "I" is a convenient fiction, which is not to say that with awakening our individuality and uniqueness are occluded. The more we are dunked in the dark waters of emptiness, the sharper and clearer our sense of the bright uniqueness of the things and beings of the world—including ourselves—becomes.

How to Meditate with "Who Am I?"

The old Japanese Zen master, Shido Munan (1603–1676) came across an old lady and asked her: "What is your koan?" She replied, "Who?"

Ask yourself, "Who am I?"

Let go of ideas and preconceptions and set aside other matters to investigate this most essential one. Whatever arises by way of an answer, let go of that too, and continue to ask, "Who am I?"

Persevere regardless, even and most especially when nothing appears to be happening. You can shorten the question to "Who?"—which makes it easier to return to. Breathing "Who?" helps to disperse thought and settles you into a more spacious place, while asking "Who am I?" raises the vital spirit of enquiry. This combination of deep settledness and enquiring spirit helps build the vessel for your investigation into this most fundamental matter. When we meditate on "Who am I?"—and this applies in Zen practice generally—it is important to not cultivate an "observer" who "oversees" the koan, thereby creating a split between an imaginary subject who asks the question and timeless dimensionless reality itself.

There is no observer.

When you unselfconsciously engage with the koan and bring all your energy and devotion to it, you gradually become intimate with it, and it with you. Like this, the self-preoccupied observer—the "I"—disappears like a swimmer into a breaking wave.

An Experience of Awakening

I want to speak for the efficacy of the koan "Who am I?" To this end I have asked my student Dotsi Burnazova to present her experience of awakening to her true nature, which occurred when she was working on the koan "Who am I?" in a sesshin at Balingup, West Australia, in the southern spring of 2014:

I asked Ross while he was ringing his bell as I was leaving dokusan, "Why are we doing this?" He quickly replied, "So you can find out who you truly are." I was running up the steps to the dojo at the top of the hill and I could still hear the sound of the bell and his words "who you truly are," "who I *truly* am." The word "truly"... "truly" "truly" "truly"... somehow stuck to my mind and I was really absorbed by it. Suddenly all my thoughts about who I was dropped, even my feelings about who I was dropped. Everything dropped—it was empty—I realized that I JUST AM. Thoughts about myself as in, Am I beautiful? Am I ugly? Am I smart? Am I stupid? Am I good? Am I bad? All gone. Because I just am—nothing else, just that. I am not beautiful or ugly, I am not smart or stupid, I am not good or bad, I am not anything, I just am. And suddenly I could see. I realized I had been blind for forty-nine years. How could I have been blind for so long? Tears were rolling down my face.

All I wanted was to run back to Ross, bow very low and tell him what I was seeing and cry to him, how could I have been so blind for so long? And I saw someone else run down to the dokusan room while I was thinking about running back to him. I realized the moment had passed and it was too late to go to Ross. Everything around me had a different dimension. It looked like I was in a living three-dimensional painting, the trees were connected to the sky, they were suddenly so close to me, the trees, the sky; the building, the walls, the sounds of the birds, there was no distance between us at all.

The leaves were touching my face, and the breeze was dancing with me. I could see the air particles forming part of that three-dimensional moving picture and I was part of it. And I was no different than anything else around me, I was just part of it, we were all connected in one existence. And we were all the same. The trees were no different from me, the grass and the sky were no different from me, the chair I was sitting on was not different from me. I was relating to everything; I was not alone anymore.

How arrogant I was until then to think that I was something more than grass, sand and pebbles on the ground. Suddenly I had so much energy, I felt I could run across the planet earth and more without stopping. I was on the top of the world. It was magic, and the truth is that I can talk about it all day long, but I don't really have the words to describe the experience as it really was.

In the past when Ross talked about the head monk Ming who had realization and was in tears, I never knew why he was weeping. Now I know.

Eighteen months after her experience, Dotsi describes how this experience had affected her life:

First of all I would like to say that the main reason that I started meditation formally was to quieten my hyperactive obsessive mind. Right up until my experience I was still obsessing about things, although not as much as before I began to practice. However, since my experience, on those occasions where I would once have headed down the path of obsessing, I now have the ability to simply move on.

The way I see the world has changed. I am finding beauty in everything: day and night, cold and hot weather, quiet and loud, outdoors and indoors, socializing and quiet times alone. I have so much joy in each moment, in the cold and the warmth, when the sun is shining and when the storm is wild, joy in each drop of rain and every sound around me.

The way I feel about myself has changed. I'm not worried what people say or think about me anymore. When I hear people whispering, instead of automatically thinking that they are talking about me, as I used to, I just don't even entertain the thought. I'm not feeling lonely anymore. Wherever I go, there I am; whoever I am with, that is who I am with. I walk alone, but I am not alone. My idea of what friendship should be has shifted—now there is more spontaneity, rather than strict rules and conditions. My friends are the pelicans when I am kayaking, and the dirty dishes that I wash every day.

Attachments to people, places and things have become weaker and I have become so much more forgiving and yet stronger within. A sense of awareness that my opinion is just one aspect of the picture follows me at all times, even when I make strong statements.

Liberated. Liberated would be the word I would use to describe my life, if I had to use one word.

Dotsi came from Macedonia to Western Australia in 1993. She has a grown-up son and daughter. Initially, she meditated by watching her thoughts, and then for seven years she counted her breath. She is a devoted student of the Zen Way. I am grateful to Dotsi for agreeing to share her experience of seeing into her true nature. It is Dotsi's hope that her account of her experience will encourage others to take up the koan "Who am I?" and to likewise realize their true nature.

When my first teacher, Robert Aitken, came to West Australia back in 1987, he conducted a Children's Ceremony for our Sangha. In that ceremony he gave each child an exercise book with the question "Who am I?" printed on the first page, so that the children could write down their changing views of who they felt themselves to be as they were growing up. My daughter Amanda immediately wrote under Roshi's inscription: "I am a book, I am a star."

We can't eradicate the "small self" that we protect so

assiduously—and we shouldn't try to. Rather we will come to see through this strange jerry-built conception that we call "me" and discover that, finally, it too is entirely lit by the moon of enlightenment.

Although we have explored the matter of who we are primarily from the perspective of emptiness, our uniqueness is not being denied. You are you. I am me. Each of us is perfectly distinguishable, and we need to be in order to communicate and to live and to work together. And our differences and distinctiveness are surely consequential in terms of birth certificates, Internet dating, salary adjustments, and even autopsy reports—to begin a very long list.

Finally, by dint of further koan work, we will come to be able to embody, express, and ultimately forget our awakening, so fully do we live it. Seen in this way, awakening to our true nature is just the beginning.

Who are you?

INVESTIGATION 1: *What Is Your Life Koan?*

The philosopher Julius Kovesi once said: "Each human life is a proposition in the mind of God." How would you express your life as a proposition?

An example might be: "A life of service to others." Or, "A life focused on creation where what is not yet apparent is brought into being." Or, "A life of contradictions: where there is freedom, there is restriction; where restriction, freedom."

These can be starting points for discovering your life koan, or indeed, as in the last instance, a life koan in itself.

In terms of finding your life koan, the question: "What are the central dilemmas of my life?" is also a good starting point.

It is good to be dealing with questions, particularly questions without stock answers. Here are some other fundamental questions that may serve as life koans, or point you in the direction of one.

Who am I?

What am I doing here?

Does my life have a purpose?

Why do I suffer?

What would I be without my stories?

Does my life have a meaning?

When you've unearthed your life koan, sit with it, investigating it until it opens for you—perhaps for your entire life.

TONY COOTE is an architect and a senior Zen practitioner in the Sydney Zen Centre. He recounts the following story:

> An old school friend of mine was walking the Kokoda Track [in Papua New Guinea] with friends. One night they camped at this place along the track, and my friend woke up hearing someone crying "Save me, Bill." Next morning they found spent rounds of ammunition on the ground at the campsite, and later still discovered that this was a place where Australians had been killed during World War II.

Ghosts haunt particular places they were associated with in life. In Tony's story we meet the ghost of an Australian soldier dying alongside the Kokoda Track in the jungle. Maybe his companions are nearby. He calls to them unavailingly; perhaps they are dead or have moved on. The question is "How do you save that ghost?" How do we save that unsettled spirit who calls to us across the generations?

Saving the Many Beings

In the Diamond Sangha we chant "Great Vows for All"—the Four Bodhisattva Vows—at the conclusion of our services. The first of these vows is: "Though the many beings are numberless, I vow to save them." What do we mean by "saving the many beings"? In the first instance, "saving" means actively including them in our heart and mind. When we do this, we allow the world in and correspondingly let go of our self-centered concerns and preoccupations. Of course, it is easy to include people we like but more difficult to be inclusive of those we can't stand or who can't stand us and who make trouble for us. The challenge is to not put those people out of our heart, for the matter of saving the many beings is finally and fundamentally without fear or favor. More fundamentally, when we are truly awakened, we experience the other as no other than our self. In this, we are intimate with all beings.

When you accord like that, each call and each response is intimately you, yourself, and you are, in the same breath, the agent of awakening for the calling world. In this way, "Save me, Bill!" gathers us all in, both the saved and the saving. In the deepest sense we are already saved—including our various ghosts— we are already included and essentially intimate. So when we vow to save the many beings, we are vowing to embody what has been thus and so from the beginning.

Nonetheless, we can't dwell in the place of "already saved." Why not? Because, as Haku'un Yasutani (1885–

1973) said, "It is too dirty." The purity of "already saved" is the purity of the *dharmakaya*: the empty body of the Buddha in all its timeless dimensionless immensity. However, living in that empty place of "already saved" means that we have no power to release beings from their suffering (not least because we are not other than them). Living in the place of "already saved" leaves us unfit for engagement and of no earthly use to anyone. That's why Yasutani said of the dharmakaya, that it is "dirty"—with more dirt accumulating the more we cling to it.

We must pitch in and get our hands dirty. The opportunities for this are legion. With global warming the tally of life forms that are under threat of extinction is immense. We are living through what is widely known as the "sixth great extinction." A third of all amphibian species are at risk. A fifth of the globe's 5,500 known mammals are classified as endangered, threatened, or vulnerable. The current extinction rate for birds may be faster than any recorded across the 150 million years of avian evolutionary history.

Everything, everyone calls out to us, *as us*. Can we be there for them? Can we give hands and feet to the dead and walk them into places they never dreamed of going?

Ghosts

I am skeptical about the existence of ghosts—those wispy filaments of ectoplasm with their trail of cheap operatic effects. Yet, in the softest way possible—almost out of conscious reach—my experience contradicts my skepticism, for I remember meeting my father's ghost.

My partner of that time, Susan, and I had gone to stay in Kangaroo Valley, in southeast Australia. My father had had what seemed to have been a heart attack the previous week and was admitted to hospital in a serious condition. The day after, I visited him with my grown-up children, and he sat up in bed and told stories and cracked jokes. He gave us the finest of performances. Feeling that he was out of danger, I flew back to Sydney to join Susan. Early the next morning I received a telephone call from my brother to say that our father had died at 4:00 a.m. He had slipped away without a muffle of farewell, too much the gentleman to impose his dying on us. I'm sure he would have found it awkward to have his weeping family around him when he went.

I wrote the following poem. It captures the moment at the bush house in Kangaroo Valley as I came downstairs in the early afternoon:

> The light gets caught and warmed
> where you stand peacefully
> making tea.
>
> I feel no affront, no shock—
> I don't even find it strange
> that you are here with us. Does
> our ardor summon you, kindle
> a steep little gully of lights and warmth
> for you to come into?—from where?

But really you are just standing there
in your ancient maroon check jacket
making tea.

Is it a pot for three? That would be
like you, including everybody in.
Head bowed you stand there and pour . . .
At the moment I noticed it was you
steam rose from the china pot into the
window light—nothing more.

I did not think that my father's presence had anything to do with unfinished business between us.
Rather it felt more like a blessing; most especially on
my relationship with Susan, which had come at the
cost of my marriage. I felt that in his gentle way he was
including us in.

At the same time, what is unfinished can haunt us,
fostering guilt or unease that gnaws at our heart. My
wife and I had a baby boy, Stephen, who lived for only
five days. The baby's tiny grave remained unmarked
for forty-five years. In all of those years I didn't once
visit the grave, putting that matter out of my mind as
I moved on in my life. In recent years, however, I felt
the need to seek it out. After I'd visited the grave, I felt
haunted by its desolation. I spoke to my son Julian, who
is a landscape architect, and he undertook to design a
memorial headstone.

We gathered as a family, and each of us said some
words for Stephen. The occasion felt warm with a good
sense of connection. There was also some unlikely

humor: Julian and I took our family to the wrong grave, so that we thought that the stonemasons hadn't even created the headstone, let alone installed it. This made sense because they had taken a year over the project—a year of futile urgings and excuses. It turned out that we had the right grave number, but that we were in the Roman Catholic rather than the Anglican section!

Haunted by Our Past

We can be haunted by our past suffering. Why do we cling to it? Why do we cling to what uproots our delight in present circumstances? Why do we cling to our guilt? Do we feel that we are unworthy to feel the happiness that might arise if we put down the burden of our self-accusation? Do we fear that if we freed ourselves from suffering arising from our past misconduct, the new lightness and ease would be too confronting in its unfamiliarity. Perhaps we simply fear letting go of the problems haunting us, because they have now become who we think we are.

A student once asked me: "What would I be without my stories?" What a great question, and, indeed, a koan in its own right. Our stories—even our painful ones—provide us with a "self," and they give that "self" a raison d'être. This constructed self is so fragile we must devote our energies to maintaining it, fostering it, even at the cost of rehashing painful narratives.

Time to abandon such futile effort and enter this moment of ghostly calling.

How do you save that ghost?

INVESTIGATION 2: *This Moment*

This moment is mysterious, arising from unknown depths. We don't know in advance what it will be, and it doesn't come marked as past, present, or future. It will never come again. Moreover, we don't know what the next moment will be.

Our remembering unfolds now; our planning unfolds now. Our reflections on the past, as well as those on the future, unfold now—which is to say, in this moment. Our whole life gathers as this very moment. This moment holds your birth and your death; it holds the birth and death of stars.

What is your moment of right now?

You never step into the same river twice
for fresh waters are always flowing in upon you.

We step, and we do not step;
We are, and we are not.

—HERACLITUS

WHEN I WAS teaching Zen sesshins, intensive meditation retreats, in Nelson, New Zealand, I would go for
a walk during my lunch break in the hope of finding
a story for my afternoon encouragement talk—or at
least some imagery for one. One incident I remember
most vividly was a cat swimming in the Maitai River,
which is to say I saw a cat crossing a stream, gingerly
stepping from stone to stone till she reached the middle.
Then turning downstream, she effortlessly slid into the
rushing water, floated for a hundred meters or so, got
out at a little white sandy cove, and walked away.

There was my talk ready-made. When I gave it, I
invoked Heraclitus to accompany my swimming cat.
Heraclitus (c. 535–c. 475 BCE) is one of the best-known
pre-Socratic philosophers and a near-contemporary of
the Buddha. He is renowned for his two-word sum-
mation of reality: "Everything flows" (in Greek, *panta*

rhei). Only fragments of his philosophical work survive, and its isolated phrases emerge at times with matchless poetic force. By way of illustration, here (as translated by John Burnet) is Heraclitus's eternal flux made manifest as a fiery cosmos:

> This world, which is the same for all, no one of gods or men has made; but it was ever, is now, and ever shall be, an ever-living fire, now in measure flaring up, now in measure dying out.

Millions of refugees are circling the earth in search of a country to take them in; now drowning at sea, now interned in camps for years with their lives and the lives of their children destroyed, now perhaps making landfall. Heraclitus's words may also evoke the personal: now overwhelmed by thoughts, now peaceful and lucid, now frustrated, now tired, now beset by lust, now bored.

The Only Unchanging Law

Heraclitus's emphasis on the inevitability of change—"the only unchanging law is the law of change"—closely corresponds to Buddhist notions of impermanence. The latter is well expressed through the image of the mundane stream of birth and death in which all things pass away. In his poem *"Ballade des dames du temps jadis"* ("Ballad of the Ladies of Times Past") the poet François Villon—reputed to be a vagabond and a thief—penned this poignant refrain: "Where are the snows of yesteryear?" (*Mais où sont les neiges d'antan?*) Villon's refrain is also a koan.

In that spirit I ask you, "Where are the snows of yesteryear?" Joseph Heller in his celebrated novel *Catch-22* has his protagonist Yossarian—haunted by his memories of the death of his friend the tail gunner Snowden—change Villon's refrain to: "Where are the Snowdens of yesteryear?"

We can each make this phrase our own. I recall a former piano student of mine named Lucien, so for me the koan is: Where are the Luciens of three weeks ago?

Lucien was forty-one when he died, but in my heart he is forever young. I taught Lucien piano when he was in his early teens. Apart from the inevitable "Moonlight Tomato," as we affectionately nicknamed Beethoven's *Moonlight Sonata*, we did lots of improvisation. (Learning to play the piano involves a lot more than formal lessons—at least as I teach it.) Lucien was an enthusiastic participant in Impro Camps for Kids, which I directed in collaboration with other musicians, artists, poets, and teachers of circus skills. The kids ranged in age from seven to seventeen. The chaos was immense, the fatigue too. It was good for my practice, though. I remember a mother of one of the children berating me because her son hadn't learned any new violin pieces over the week, and I was able to take on her anger without becoming reactive.

I have such vivid memories of some kids stilt-walking through a lake while orchestras of improvisers, playing instruments they had invented, accompanied them from hill slopes under gauzy blue flags. Meanwhile the unicyclists rode up and down red, blue, and yellow freshly painted bedsheets, and the poets chanted poems they'd received serendipitously from the surrealist parlor game called "Exquisite Corpse."

Lucien would join in all the improvisations, and at night he would perform Beethoven and Chopin for us all on the electric piano we'd brought along—less than satisfactory for the glorious music and a challenge for Lucien to play.

In the piano lessons I gave in those years I would introduce students to John Cage's revolutionary 1952 piece 4'33" (rather than Chopin's *Revolutionary Etude* of 1831). The student would enter, and I would be seated at the piano without playing or moving for 4'33". I would then turn around and ask the student what they had experienced, or more precisely, "What was the performance?" Many responded, "The performance was the sounds—of traffic, crows, breathing, my house creaking, easing its back in midsummer heat"—which was Cage's idea in 4'33" (or "four-foot-thirty-three inches," as he liked to joke). Indeed, wherever you are, whatever you are doing, 4'33" is always in session. When I performed 4'33" for Lucien, I asked him: "What was the performance?" He replied, "The piece of music I imagined."

In more recent years Lucien would come over to my place and play works from the classical canon such as Liszt's immensely challenging Sonata in B Minor. I had nothing to teach him, and I could only admire what he was doing, encourage him, and request him to play more.

On his last visit, Lucien brought me the gift of a copy of Rachmaninoff's "Daisies"—unattached crumpled sheets covered with pencil markings—and said, "Ross, if you play this, you can smell the earth the rain and the flowers so strongly, you can almost taste them."

The news of Lucien's death from cancer was shocking, unbelievable. He came home from the hospital because the chemo treatment was "working so well," but he actually came home to die. I chanted the *"Enmei Jukku Kannon Gyo"*—the ten-verse sutra of timeless life—for him, and composed a piece for him called "You Can Taste the Rain" in the late Romantic style that he loved. At the funeral, Lucien's body was in a wicker coffin close to the piano. His eldest brother, Nathan, a dear friend and artistic collaborator of mine, said in his eulogy: "Although Lucien's life was brief, it was complete—and it touched so many people, including his own students."

Lucien's brother Kynan had scanned photographs of Lucien from his babyhood, childhood, adolescence, and beyond, onto a video that showed Lucien goofing off, playing with the family cat, and giving his first piano recital. Throughout the video I was playing Bach preludes on an out-of-tune piano on which many of the notes were not working. ("Bach on a Ruined Piano?"— Lucien would have appreciated that.) I played on, as the images of Lucien, including one with him standing on his head, evoked special times in his life. As the final prelude was nearing its conclusion, I looked up and saw on the screen a note in Lucien's hand: "Thank you for everything. Love, Lucien." Everything—the images, the candles, the fractured music, his grieving family and friends, his eldest brother's moving eulogy—conveyed his presence, indeed was him.

Fresh Waters Are Always Flowing In Upon You

The moment is timelessly vast, encompassing our birth and our death, and the birth and death of stars; yet in the same breath it flows, and it is in this latter sense that Heraclitus wrote that you never step in the same river twice—for fresh waters are always flowing in upon you. It is not just that the waters flowing in are fresh; *you yourself are ever changing and in constant flux.* Every sixteen days, about 72 percent of our bodily atoms are replaced. Whatever or whoever you conceive yourself to be, that *you* is adrift in a sea of change—is indeed that sea of change. Even though we operate from a core conception of ourselves—thinking we know perfectly well who we are—we are a network of relations with others and with the world at large that is in constant flux.

Childbirth, and the months of sleeplessness that follow, over time are blessedly forgotten, or may be at least hard to summon up. So much of our experience is like this; even intense intimacy such as we experience through meditation, making love, being in nature, or listening to music, ends up in that soft avalanche into oblivion—or, what my fellow Zen teacher Arthur Wells calls "the forgetory."

The Dialectic of Time and Timelessness

We step, and we do not step;
We are, and we are not.

"We step," summons up the world of contingency, of impermanence: birth and death, advancing and retreating, confidence and trepidation. "We do not step," on the other hand, evokes the timeless realm where there is no birth and death, no advancing or retreating, and neither courage nor trepidation. Regarding "we are, and we are not," "we are" pays tribute to our uniqueness, our singularity; "we are not" acknowledges the boundlessness of our true nature. "We step" and "we do not step," and "we are" and "we are not" present the horns of a dilemma. We take "being" and "nonbeing" for granted—especially the former in these materialistic times. But being and nonbeing present a dichotomy, an apparent paradox to be dissolved. So how do you step beyond them and experience liberation?

Moreover:

How is it that you can never step into the same river twice?

INVESTIGATION 3: *What Is Time?*

When the great twentieth-century physicist Richard Feynman met a group of schoolchildren and one of them asked him, "What is time?" he answered with another question: "What if there is no such thing as time? What then?"

"What is time?" is a koan, surely.

In Zen, while we acknowledge the passage of time and our own passing, we are encouraged to focus on the present moment as all there is, as the only place where we can experience our own life, as well as reality at large. As the twentieth-century Zen teacher Joko Beck put it: "Nothing has ever existed except this moment." The passage of time and the primacy of the moment both play to the big theme of "What is time?"

Saint Augustine of Hippo (354–430) claimed he understood time very well—until he tried to explain what it was. Then he was completely at a loss. Augustine's experience is familiar to Zen students everywhere when they are stuck on a koan. You don't know, and you don't know. Then you settle into that not knowing and continue to ask the question, regardless, carrying it with you day and night.

James Gleick writes, in *Time Travel: A History*:

We know that time is imperceptible. We know that it is immaterial. We cannot see it, hear it, or touch it. If people say they perceive the passing of time, that's just a figure of speech that they're picking up on. The ticking of the clock, the beating of your heart. . . . Whatever time is, it lies outside the grasp of our senses.

The nature of being human is to experience time, moment by moment, rather than all at once. However, through the practice of the Zen Way we may experience intimations of a timeless reality that transcends the steady parade of moments in clock time, such that we find accord with lines from the Zen tradition such as Wumen Huikai's "Eternity is in the now."

What about Feynman's response to the child: "What if there is no such thing as time?" If that is so, what is it that our clocks are actually measuring with ever-increasing accuracy? If there is no such thing as time, what difference does that make to our lives? It is difficult, perhaps impossible, to talk of the change we experience without invoking the concept of time. In that regard, the concept of time is clearly vital for navigating our personal and social lives, as well as, on a global scale, for science, politics, and travel. However, does time have a substantive reality? Is there such a thing as time?

We assuredly live our lives as if there is such a thing as time; the steady parade of birthdays, weddings, and funerals in our lives bear witness to this. However, in moments of absorption or in sudden insight we may experience timelessness, and if we commit to the Way, we slowly come to embody this experience, learn its expression—even as it is inexpressible—and mature it through our practice and our life. Dongshan's beautiful line: "In the time and season of cause and effect, it quietly illuminates" bears witness to the timelessness of our deepest nature.

Through the exploration of the varying yet indissoluble relationship between time and timelessness to follow, and its intimate connection to who we are, I ask you:

What is time?

When You're Making Love, Who Is the Other? 6

SEX IS SO coupled with fantasy and imagination and correspondingly hooked into the depths of our psyche. As sexual beings, we encounter the endless pitfalls and pratfalls, as well as the loss of dignity that comes with the territory. Over a lifetime as sexual beings we are all vulnerable to sexual desire. It is said that not even ninety-year-olds are safe.

Eros for the Way and sexual desire readily entangle. I remember in my first sesshin during the rounds of *kinhin* when participants walk in meditation around the perimeter of the dojo, I was entranced by the hair and nape of the neck of a young woman in front of me. For seven days, kinhin after kinhin, I trailed her on aching legs, as she receded through high mountain mists.

The Passions Are Enlightenment

A central theme of traditional Buddhism is that in order to get enlightened we must cut off the passions. However, that isn't the Zen Way. Here's an exchange between the old teacher Zhaozhou Congshen (778–897) and a monk that makes this clear. "Buddhahood" here is understood to mean enlightenment:

> Zhaozhou said, "Passion is Buddhahood; Buddhahood is passion."
>
> A monk asked, "How do we get rid of the passions?"
>
> Zhaozhou replied, "Why get rid of the passions?"

Why indeed? The passions—including sexual passion—are a part of who we truly are, no less than blood, bone, breath, earth, and sky. The passions are expressive of the Way and, indeed, not other than it. In terms of living the Way, we neither cut off the passions, nor indulge them. Just be there for them, as them.

More radically, the Zen teacher Songyuan Chongyue (1139–1209) emphasized that unless we can face up to the fact that sex and sexuality are intrinsic to our nature, we cannot truly experience liberation:

> In order to realize the Way with perfect clarity, there is one essential point you must penetrate and not avoid: the red thread of passion that cannot be severed. Few really face this problem, and it is not at all easy to settle. Face it directly without hesitation, for how else can liberation come?

In the Diamond Sangha tradition in which I teach, Songyuan's words are fashioned into a koan: "Why is it that perfectly enlightened saints and bodhisattvas cannot cut off the vermillion thread?" Vermillion was the color of women's undergarments in old China, and accordingly was linked with sexual desire. The vermillion thread was also called "the line of tears," evoking the sadness that is sometimes entangled with sexual desire and its consummation. The "line of tears" also points more broadly to the truth that the one who loves, suffers.

It may be that Zen rarely mentions love because it has so much respect for it. By love, here, I mean compassion and loving-kindness, of course, but also the Eros that drives the Way: the red thread of passion that fosters the generativity that gets the teaching passed on. On the lineage chart given to the new Zen teacher at Dharma transmission, the names of the teachers—generation upon generation of them going back to the Buddha—are joined by inky red lines and curves, which return to, and emanate from, a red circle representing the empty world.

However, in Zen's monastic traditions there is almost complete silence around sex and sexuality. This may be because monks and nuns took precepts prohibiting them from engaging in sexual activity—which is not to suggest for a moment that they did not. Unfortunately, misogyny, together with denial and cover-up, may also be a reason why there's so little attention devoted to sex and sexuality in the traditional koan literature.

In our lay traditions we have an opportunity, indeed a responsibility, to include sex and sexuality as part of the Dharma as it is unfolding in the West—an important reason for this book. After all, sex and sexuality play a vital role in our lives, beyond being our means to have children, by helping us to come to know our partners and ourselves in depth: to bond and become intimate with them.

I remember hearing a radio program on sexuality where the guest speaker talked about addressing a crowd of undergraduates and a girl saying that she felt trepidation at the prospect of entering a sexual relationship. In this age when everything concerning sex and sexuality is so garishly and explicitly presented over the Internet, it was touching to hear about this girl expressing her vulnerability. To be in a sexual relationship is to be vulnerable. We allow ourselves to be known in our neediness and, accordingly, in depth. Desire and fear are very close. We fear losing the one we desire, and so we fear committing ourselves, for we may end up abandoned.

When we're in love, we see our beloved everywhere: in changing light, in a mountain, in a flight of birds, and in our own smile. We see things through his or her eyes too: "That's how my beloved would see it." We know this unerringly. As our relationship deepens, we get to find out how different the other can be— sometimes to our dismay. Their differing needs and wants, as well as their contrariness, can emerge as confronting. This can be part of the loss of illusion we feel when the novelty of the relationship wears off and we find that our wants and needs don't accord as they used to seem to. I have to say that the depth and joy of sexual connection established early on can continue to nourish a relationship when it enters difficult periods; even the memory of past sexual intimacy can do this.

Of course, in making love we're aware of the other *as other*, and as we give ourselves over to meeting their needs, we lose our fixation on having our own needs met—while finding that they mostly get met anyway. Finally, any clinging to "self" and "other" may yield to the surrender of orgasm and the sweet release following.

At the same time, the other is not other than ourselves, and making love opens us up to this over and again. Self and other vanish into the mutuality and power of sexual union, and although privacy and passion are crucial for making love, in this pucker of time we call "now" the night sky with its countless stars is gathered into our embrace—even as it gathers us in.

When you're making love, who is the other?

INVESTIGATION 4: *"It is like—"*

Vladimir Nabokov, near the end of his great novel *Ada* (an exploration of time and love if ever there was one), has his heroine say:

> I wonder if the attempt to discover those things is worth the stained glass. We can know the time, we can know a time. We can never know Time. Our senses are simply not meant to perceive it. It is like—

What is Time like? Better still, what is it?

On Birth 7

I FOUND IT difficult to begin a chapter on birth and delayed for a time, messing with other matters in order to put off commencing. Perhaps it is difficult to talk about birth because it seems to be somehow linked to feelings of shame, or at least that is my experience. Sometimes it is confronting to imagine our mother giving birth to us, just as it may be challenging to imagine our parents having sex.

"What is your source and origin?" is certainly a viable koan, and the response is most often assumed to be vast emptiness in its unknowability. What is mostly passed over is the karmic account of our source and origin; to the effect that we are born from our mother's womb, most likely entering the world through her vagina. There is a story about the Japanese Zen master Ikkyū Sojun (1394–1481) that puts this matter in its proper perspective:

> When Ikkyu was traveling he saw a naked woman bathing in a river. He bowed to her three times in the direction of her vagina. Several passersby asked him for an explanation.
>
> "Why did you bow to her pussy?" he was asked.
>
> He responded, "Women are the treasure house of Buddhism, they are the source out of which

every being comes forth, including the Buddha and Bodhidharma."

And they nourished us into life and sustained us when we couldn't fend for ourselves—all of which deserves our deepest respect.

Birth is surely a benchmark for pain and endurance. And surely a woman emerges changed, even transformed, on the other side, perhaps in some measure dying to the person she was before. The juggernaut of giving birth, with its accompanying pain, is just the beginning of the joy and pain of raising a child, where she grows great with allowing—and restraining.

Arthur Wells, who teaches Zen in Christchurch, New Zealand, wrote to me movingly of the birth of his grandchild Emma. In the concluding lines of his letter, he gives an intimate account of his experience of the Way, following Emma's birth:

Dear Ross,

Today Jessie gave birth to baby Emma, after a 20-hour labor. Elisabeth and I were with her, massaging her feet and hands and shoulders, while Paul, her husband, gave untiring, loving encouragement . . . I am sure that baby Emma was distressed too, experiencing the same long ordeal from the inside.

Why does birth have to be so painful? I asked myself, and the Darwinian answer is the only one that comes back—it is so painful because we stood up on two feet and grew very big heads that don't fit down through a narrow pelvis evolved for four-legged locomotion. Nobody planned this. Absolutely no one is to blame.

Being there with Jessie for Emma's birth left me with huge awe for my own mother and for Elisabeth's brave efforts in giving birth to Robin and Jessie. At the end of it all Jessie wept for joy to have her baby on her tummy.

Like Zhaozhou's "mind" being pure cat when he walks out with his sandal on his head, my own mind tonight is nothing but a tiny pink ape, snuffling for its mother's breast and pattering perfect little hands on her face and chest—just that vision over and over of Jessie exhausted but radiant, and tiny Emma alive and well.

The Koan

Why does birth have to be so painful? I asked myself again and again, and the Darwinian answer is the only one that comes back—it is so painful because we stood up on two feet and grew very big heads that don't fit down through a narrow pelvis evolved for four-legged locomotion. Nobody planned this. Absolutely no one is to blame.

The essential point here is neither in Arthur's Darwinian account of the pain of birth, nor in his brief and cogent ensuing lines: "Nobody planned this.

Absolutely no one is to blame." Though I am grateful for his perspective.

What is our true nature transcending Darwinism, theology, and their disputes?

INVESTIGATION 5: *Child's Play*

For a child, getting to know their name, gender, and role in the family is vital for their developing sense of identity, and these can be explored through the question "Who are you?" However, in the right circumstances, opening the question up and asking, "Who are you, *really*?" may be helpful for raising a child's curiosity about their deepest nature, and indeed the deepest nature of us all.

Imagination and lightness of touch are key. What is playful—as when the child turns herself into a dragon or a crocodile—may also be deep. It's great to play along, meeting them where they are and assuming ever-changing guises for their delight. Thus you truly meet.

What is true meeting in child's play?
In such a meeting: Who are they?
And who are you?

"Mum, What Is Time?" 8

BRITTA BIEDERMANN, a student of the Zen Way, told me a story that illustrates how much we quantify and commodify time.

Riding in a "silent carriage" of a high-speed commuter train in Germany, a little girl focusing intensely on her coloring-in book all of sudden lifts her head and asks her mum in a relatively clear and loud voice: "Mama, what is time?"(*Mama, was ist Zeit?*). The other passengers all lift their heads too at this point, stopping their business as they wait for the mother's response. . . . After a long pause the mother laughs and responds, "That is a good question. It is something you have less and less of the older you get."

We are always quantifying time: we have time, we don't have time, time is running out. Time, taken on these terms, is a commodity; the sentiment "Time is money" expresses this succinctly.

It is significant that the people in the "silent carriage" on the long white sleek ICE train, traveling from one end of Germany to the other in seven hours, are trying to save time, to catch up on time, to use time to accomplish their tasks—all the while being oblivious to the world outside. This aptly expresses the commodification of time and the narrow moment of utterly focused attention on the laptop's screen that supports such commodification; that is, until a little girl disperses it with her question. It is such a confronting question, you can practically hear that profound silence before the little girl's mother replies, "That is a good question. It is something you have less and less of the older you get."

Truly the moment is timeless. Even to call it "the moment" is to create a convenient fiction. Children ask "What is time?" but for the most part are unconcerned about knowing the time, though "only three sleeps to your birthday" certainly has meaning!

Back in 1973, Michael Ende wrote a marvelous novel for children called *Momo*. Actually *Momo* is a novel for us all, for it addresses a central issue of our time: why, when we have so many time-saving appliances and instant digital access to the world (think of how much time it used to take to post a letter!), do we seem to have so little time?

A question such as "How much time do I have?" can be hugely consequential for ourselves and for our families, though. I think of the situation of being told we have a terminal illness. How do we use the time we have left? Perhaps it is an opportunity to forgive, to seek forgiveness, and to tell people that we love them—while we still can.

An endless life may well be a meaningless one, but the fact that we will die, perhaps imminently, gives urgency, even meaning, to our life.

In *Momo*, Michael Ende makes a wonderful observation regarding time:

Life holds one great but commonplace mystery . . . time. Calendars and clocks exist to measure time, but that signifies little because we all know that an hour can seem an eternity or pass in a flash, according to how we spend it. Time is life itself, and life resides in the human heart.

The mother's remarks point to the familiar sense of time seeming to speed up as we age. Again, being there for what is, being intimate with what presents, shifts our apprehension of time from an exclusive focus on how much time we have—or don't have—to a greater intimacy with the timelessness of this moment, right here, right now.

What is time?

If that little girl had asked you, how would you have responded?

INVESTIGATION 6: *The Nature of the Self and Time*

Who are we?

What is the "I" that each of us feels endures through the passage of time and change? The nature of the self and the nature of time are surely enmeshed, such that when we encounter our true nature and walk that awakening into the depths of our life, we find that our experience of time changes correspondingly. We no longer feel so confined in the cage of clock time, and, as we realize our intimacy with the whole of reality, we experience the moment as all encompassing: not less than the universe itself. Yet in the face of that immensity, we continue to make and to keep our appointments.

Why, when we are wholly unrestricted, do we observe these forms?

Eduardo Galeano's "True Contemporaries" 9

In *The Book of Embraces*, Uruguayan author Eduardo Galeano introduces us to poet Juan Gelman and the question of true contemporaries:

> "Who are my contemporaries?" Juan Gelman asks himself. Juan says that sometimes he comes across men who smell of fear—in Buenos Aires, Paris, or anywhere in the world—and feels that these men are not his contemporaries. But there is a Chinese who, thousands of years ago, wrote a poem about a goatherd who is far from his beloved and yet can hear in the middle of the night, in the middle of the snow, the sound of her comb running through her hair. And reading this distant poem, Juan finds that, yes, these people—the poet, the goatherd, and the woman—are truly his contemporaries.

The Koan

However hurt and shattered one might be, one can always find true contemporaries anywhere in time. Who are your true contemporaries?

Eduardo Hughes Galeano (1940–2015) was a Uruguayan journalist, writer, and novelist, as well as being a champion of the Left who fought for the liberation of oppressed people in Latin America. He was considered to be "global soccer's preeminent man of letters" and regarded by some as a literary giant of the Latin American Left. I've carried Galeano's *Book of Embraces* with me over the years, drawing on his prose poems and brief stories for Dharma talks and teishos, as well as recommending his book to students. We can get a sense of the Dharma as it plays out in Galeano's book, especially in his concluding piece titled "The Gust":

The wind whistles within me.

I am naked. Master of nothing, master of no one, not even of my own convictions. I am my face in the wind, against the wind, and I am the wind that strikes my face.

The intimacy of wind and person, conveyed from diverse angles, perfectly conveys the Way, and it is indeed a viable koan.

In that spirit I ask you: "If that is Galeano, who are you?"

Juan Gelman was born in Buenos Aires in 1930 and died in Mexico City in 2014. A celebrated poet—his published output includes more than twenty books of poetry—Gelman, like Galeano, was a committed human rights activist. Exiled from Argentina after the military coup of 1976, he lived in Europe, the United States, and Mexico, where he ultimately settled. In 1976, his daughter Nora Eva, age nineteen; his son Marcelo Ariel, age twenty; and his pregnant daughter-in-law Maria Claudia, age nineteen, were kidnapped from their home, becoming three of the 30,000 *desaparecidos*—the people who "vanished" during the reign of the right-wing military junta.

Nora Eva survived, but Gelman's son and daughter-in-law were killed. In 1990 Gelman was taken to identify his son's remains—he had been executed and buried in a barrel filled with sand and cement—and years later, in 2000, he was able to trace his grand-daughter, born in a backdoor hospital before Maria Claudia's murder and given to a pro-government family in Uruguay. The remains of Maria Claudia have not yet been recovered.

In the face of such tragedy, we can only imagine how shattered and heartbroken Gelman must have been. In the face of his struggles and the agonies of his life, we can understand why he may have sought, and found, contemporaries elsewhere in time.

Yet consolation is not the chief theme here, important and understandable as it is. Rather it is *intimacy across time* that is in play. Distance and duration have no purchase here, for when we realize who we truly are, the gap between past and present dissolves in the softest of avalanches, and there is no time barrier at all. This is the timeless intimacy evoked by Wumen Huikai in his commentary on the first case of *The Gateless Barrier* (as translated by Robert Aitken):

When you pass through the barrier of the gate-less gate, you will not only interview Zhaozhou intimately, you will walk hand in hand with the ancestral teachers in the successive generations of our lineage—the hair of their eyebrows entangled with yours, seeing with the same eyes, hearing with the same ears. Won't that be fulfilling?

With this encounter, the old teachers live in us, as us; they are our true contemporaries, as we are theirs.

Intimacy across Time

In Eduardo Galeano's "Art and Time," the sound of the woman's comb running through her hair casts such a net of intimacy across the centuries. It dissolves the distance between the goatherd and his beloved. It disperses the time barrier between the unnamed Chinese poet living who knows when and the twentieth-century Argentinian poet Juan Gelman; between the unnamed Chinese poet and Galeano recounting Gelman's story, and us reading it in the twenty-first century. The poetry of this small intimate act carries such depth and resonance.

My first teacher, Robert Aitken, once said to me: "The Way is grounded in genuine experience and poetry." In the light of his words, the poetic image of the beloved's comb going through her hair "in the middle of the night, in the middle of the snow" evokes the unfathomable experience of who we truly are: words heard or read so deeply, so intensely, that everything else vanishes. Such experiences are timeless, and they defy adequate description.

Presence, Attention, Love

Conventional wisdom has it that, although we have memories and records of the past of varying reliability, the past is gone. Moreover, the future is not yet, and can only be guessed at. Accordingly, I have unbounded admiration for people who plan their future in great detail—it takes courage to drive pylons into airy nothingness and to plan minutely what can't remotely be foreseen. Regarding the future, any sense that we live on after we die finds conventional expression as: we live on for a time in the memories of our families and others who know us until the last time someone speaks our name or thinks of us—and we finally die.

Earlier we learned of the fate of Gelman's son and daughter-in-law and the appalling suffering that their tragic end must have occasioned him and his family. None of us is proof against such a tragedy, and it is surely important to attend to those who come into our lives while we still have time. Love is forged and fostered through such attention, not only romantically, but in broader, grittier ways. Such intimate connection arises from the attention we give people and how we support them, as expressed at the conclusion of Gelman's poem "End," as translated by Professor Ilan Stavans:

Poetry is a way of living.
Look at the people at your side.
Do they eat? Suffer? Sing? Cry?
Help them fight for their hands, their eyes,
    their mouth, for the kiss to
kiss and the kiss to give away, for their table,
    their bread, their letter a
and their letter h, for their past—were they not
    children?—for their
present, for the piece of peace, of history and
    happiness that belongs to
them, for the piece of love, big, small, sad, joy,
    that belongs to them and
is taken away in the name of what, of what?
Your life will then be an innumerable river to
    be called pedro, juan,
ana, maria, bird, lung, the air, my shirt, violin,
    sunset, stone, that
handkerchief, old waltz, wooden horse.
Poetry is this.
Afterward, write it.

Finding Our True Contemporaries through Writing

"Why does one write, if not to put one's pieces together?"
—EDUARDO GALEANO

Writing connects us to our depths and steers us towards a more inclusive, generous vision of the world, so that we come to empathize with others across temporal and cultural barriers, even alien ones. As with meditation, writing can help us to open our heart to the plight of others, giving us access to the thoughts and emotions of the dispossessed, the wounded, and the dying. This was surely the impulse that drove the work of social activists such as Galeano and Gelman. By writing—and reading—we are opened up, and the distance between us and teeming, suffering humanity shrinks. Imaginative identification, moral imagination, or empathy—call it what you will—helps to connect us to others, regardless of color or creed. The literary critic Geordie Williamson writes:

> The dignity and fraternity that we grant others by our imaginative and empathetic attentions is universal or it is nothing. *Homo sum humani a me alienum pulo*—"I am human and nothing of that which is human is alien to me"—wrote Roman playwright Terence more than two millennia ago. What is less known about Terence is that he was a Berber. He was a brown-skinned citizen of the Republic.

We fear what is alien, yet we give it a home in our heart, as our heart. Like this, we deepen in the Way as we learn to include more of the suffering of the world, as well as our own. When we enter the moment fully—the moment of fear, the moment of repugnance—we discover that the suffering of others that is so often confronting is our true face and home.

The Timeless Moment

Let us return to the notion of true contemporaries. There is the sense that our true contemporaries—no matter how distant in time they may be—come to life as poetry or music in this moment arising from unknowable depths. Our lives too, with our falling in and out of love, are eternity's opportunity and its song. Although the music unfolds in time, immersed, we lose our sense of time's passage. In music in particular, time is permeable, and we are permeable. My old piano teacher Alice Carrard ("Madame," as her students called her), was perhaps the finest classical pianist who ever lived in my home city of Perth, Western Australia. She was a fierce teacher, and it was a battle to get to the second bar of a Mozart sonata without being pulled up. As my hands descended towards the opening chord, she would cry, "Not like that!" "Not like that" has become my three-word teaching, most especially in dokusan.

The deeper we live the Way, the more our conventional notions of time are nudged towards the edges of our experience. Time is inexorable, granted, and surely sickness, old age, and death bear down. And yet past, present, and future are increasingly gathered into this puckering of time we call "now," which is no other than our true face and home. When we experience like this, we come into our own, and "our own," beyond any ownership, is immeasurable.

Genuine realization transcends time and culture, and it is by its nature timeless. No need to throw away our watches though; punctuality is the courtesy of kings and queens. But within the flux there is a mystery.

Who are your true contemporaries?

The Crow Flies Backwards 10

A crow cries: and the world unrolls like a blanket;
like a worn bush blanket, charred at the horizons.
—RANDOLPH STOW

CROWS ARE MY constant companions. I can hear their *caaark* even as I write this line. I stare out my study window, and there they are in my huge cape lilac tree— big, black, sleek. Whenever I take myself too seriously, I hear their call and am brought back to earth. Crows are scavengers; they are also highly intelligent: one will fly down and lift the lid of the garbage bin, then the other will go in and help herself to whatever may be inside. Then they fly off and share the spoils.

This is crow country, where the Nyoongar people, for whom crows have powerful spiritual significance, have lived for more than forty thousand years. The Nyoongar people adopt animal totems, whom they regard as spiritual siblings and for whom they take responsibility. If you are born Nyoongar, you'll be either *wardong* the crow or *manach* the white cockatoo.

The following story gives us a sense of how strongly the Nyoongar people identify with the crow. It was told by a Nyoongar elder in 1989, during the year-long Aboriginal protest against the redevelopment of the former Swan Brewery on a sacred site of

powerful significance to the Nyoongar people—called
Goonininup—a place where the Waugal, a snakelike
Dreamtime creature who was responsible for the cre-
ation of the Swan and Canning Rivers, went in:

> "That building there, there was hundreds of
> crows. They all flew there and they all sat cry-
> ing wicked. That's the first time in my life I seen
> hundreds of crows in one spot, especially on a
> building . . . any Nyungah can tell you . . . even a
> Wajella ("white feller") . . . you usually only see 5
> or 4 only . . . I heard them. I seen them. I couldn't
> believe so many crows in one group. Black cock-
> atoos yes, but not crows."
>
> Another Nyoongar elder said: "That's the
> blackfellas coming."

Nyoongar language is the sound of country. A strik-
ing instance of this is the Nyoongar word for "crow"—
wardong. You can hear the call of the crow in that
word—*waaaaaaaardong*. I am honored to have been
able to learn this and other aspects of Nyoongar culture from Michael Wright, a Nyoongar man who sits
with the Zen Group of Western Australia. Michael is
encouraging all of us to bear witness to the Nyoongar people by sitting on country and meeting Nyoongar elders, as a way of beginning to heal the suffering
brought about by the British invasion of their country.
The crows are keepers of country here, and the
crow's *caaark* is a reminder to come home to our true
home in its vastness.

When you hear a crow call, who is hearing that sound?

"The Land Where the Crow Flies Backwards"

In Australia, the expression "the land where the crow flies backwards" refers to the remote outback, or more generally to any strange place. It derives from the cattle country of southwest Queensland, or the country "back of Bourke" in northern New South Wales, in Eastern Australia. The expression may be of Aboriginal origin, for many of the drovers and stockmen were Aboriginal men.

The expression "crows fly backwards" was popularized by Aboriginal country singer Dougie Young from South West Queensland in his song "The Land Where the Crows Fly Backwards," which he recorded in 1963. In 1963 or '64 Jeremy Beckett, an anthropologist, made field recordings of Young, several of which were released in 1965 as an EP called *The Land Where the Crows Fly Backwards* (Wattle). Here is the stanza that refers to the phrase:

> When it comes to ridin' horses
> or workin' cattle, I've mixed with the very best,
> in the land where the crows fly backwards
> and the pelican builds his nest.

"The land where the crow flies backwards" is a fine example of traditional Australian argot, which is backwards, upside down, and often mocking. Although such speech is grounded in commonsense culture, it can be wildly imaginative: "mad as a cut snake" means very angry and upset, or just plain insane; "flat out like a lizard drinking" means working hard, under pressure; "a dog's breakfast" means a complete mess. "Stone the crows!" is an expression of shock and annoyance, because crows are unwelcome guests on sheep stations, where, given the chance, they kill and eat newborn lambs. "The sheep are out in the long paddock" means the sheep are out on the road; "the sheep are in the sky paddock" means they're dead.

The Story of June Rose

I will now tell the true story of June Rose and how "the land where the crow flies backwards" got her expelled from school. June Rose was born in Rangoon, Burma, in 1932. Her mother, Ma Lat, was Burmese royalty. Her father, Herbert Bellamy—an Australian business-man with interests in horseracing—told June Rose yarns about his time in the Australian bush and read her Henry Lawson's poems. June Rose would tell her friends: "I can tell you everything about Kalgoorlie and the Southern Cross; I can tell you about the half-bald cockatoo in the pub in whose cup people would pour beer, and when the parrot was sloshed he'd say, 'Give me another feather and I'll fly.'"

In February 1942, when June Rose was nine, the family's idyll ended. Japanese bombers raided Rangoon as the prelude to occupation, and the family was evacuated to India. This is where our story picks up:

At eleven, June Rose was sent to a convent school at

Kalimpong, in West Bengal, where her father's influence was her downfall. A nun who clearly looked down on mixed-race children was giving a geography lesson about Australia and sarcastically asked June Rose if she'd left anything off the map on the blackboard. June Rose got up from her desk, walked to the blackboard, and put a dot in the center of the map of Australia. "Baragarawindy," she told the class, "is dream country; it is the land of opposites: the rivers flow inland instead of out, the leaves grow upwards instead of down, the snakes have feathers, and the crows fly backwards to keep the dust out of their eyes." She was expelled.

"Baragarawindy" would seem to be straight out of June's imagination—in a literal sense, there seems to be no such place—and her language is the language of emptiness, where opposites unite in a realm of neither forwards nor backwards, north nor south; a realm where contradictions thrive.

How do you inhabit that dimensionless space where the crow flies backwards?

INVESTIGATION 7: *The Present Moment*

The past is gone. The future is not yet. All we have is the present moment. That's all that's on offer, our only home. In the same breath, the present moment is that infinitesimal point where the past becomes the future, and the future turns into the past. How can we live there? Seen thus, the present moment has no reality at all, and we live and die, dance and love on nothing at all.

How can this be?

IT IS SAID that Shakyamuni Buddha during his long vigil under the bodhi tree sat with the koan, "Why do we suffer?" Surely he sought a path that would lead to our release from the suffering and anguish of sickness, old age, and death. After all, these were the issues that had pressed him to seek enlightenment in the first place.

With his awakening, which occurred when he looked up and saw the morning star, the Buddha is said to have exclaimed: "Now I see that all beings are the Tathagata; it is just their delusions and attachments that prevent them from bearing witness to it." The Tathagata is the one who is intimate with the whole of reality, beyond all considerations of coming and going. By referring to himself as the Tathagata, the Buddha avoided the personal pronoun "I" with its limiting implications. It is as though the scope and profundity of his experience demanded a new, though still inadequate, designation.

On seeing the morning star, Shakyamuni realized the Way, and with that profound experience, he understood why we suffer and how we might find release from our suffering.

Why Do We Suffer?

In terms of the Mahayana teachings, we suffer because we are ignorant of the nature of reality and our relation to it. In particular, we suffer because we are caught up in dualistic conceptions of self and other. Concerning this, Haku'un Yasutani pointed out that the fundamental delusion of humanity is well expressed as "I am in here, you are out there."

Inherently, we all share in the Buddha's enlightenment; at the deepest level it is also our own. However, the tangled forest of our delusions and attachments regarding who we are and our relation to the world shuts out the vastness and light of our true nature, and we suffer as we cultivate a self that isn't there, opposing it to the world as we compete for what we already have in abundance.

The Range of Suffering and Its Release

The word *suffering* encompasses a wide range of human experience: everything from the appalling pain of cancer all the way down to the niggling dissatisfactions we feel with our lives. I want to make it clear that I am not claiming that the suffering experienced in cancer is the outcome of our delusions about reality. I am also cautious about claiming that when we realize and experience the dropping away of our delusions about the nature of reality, this would necessarily affect the course of our cancer or even be of much assistance in dealing with the extremities of its pain.

Charles de Gaulle said that old age is a shipwreck. As we age, we are more prone to illness. The longer we live, the more of death there is and the clearer the apprehension that we ourselves will inevitably die. We may also lose the sense of who we are in the long good-bye of Alzheimer's disease: a death before the fact.

All that said, we *can* deal with our pain in measure and find release from our suffering by going the course with it, bringing our attention to it, holding it in our attention, and allowing it. This is how we deal with our physical pain in measure, as well as with our emotional pain running the gamut from irritation all the way to profound grief.

Through it all, though, we do spend a lot of time unnecessarily sweating the small stuff. I think of my own indignation, touchiness, and rancor: emotions I am not proud of and ashamed to own. I think, "I should be better than this," and this in turn brings up my shame, with its own suffering. We are all vulnerable on these fronts—and also to the pangs of envy and of not being valued to our own estimation.

My first accordion teacher, Harry Bluck, used to say: "You can't insult me—I've been insulted by experts." In the 1950s he would stay up all night, drinking Turkish coffee and chain-smoking Rothman's cork-tip cigarettes as he wrote arrangements for an eighteen-piece dance band. When the parts were given out in the radio station's recording studio, the musicians would mutter, "Who wrote this crap?" He told me, "Well that hurt, but at least it got them a job."

Just that disappointment. Taking it on—allowing,

allowing, allowing—that's how we live the Way: just disappointment all through, just humiliation all through.

A Life without Suffering

A life without suffering would be meaningless. Without suffering there would be no need for empathy or for mutual support, and there would be no spur to realize who we truly are. I don't wish suffering on anybody, nor do I see any special virtue in suffering for its own sake; nonetheless, if I were offered the opportunity to live a life without suffering, I would refuse that offer.

There are tragedies in our lives, as well as in the lives of those we love, and on these occasions grief and deep questioning as to *why*—when we feel that we have treated others well and lived a good life—we should be visited by such appalling suffering is understandable and not less than the Way itself.

When we realize that the other is no other than our self—and this is at the core of the Buddha's experience under the bodhi tree—we are released from our separation from others and from reality at large. With this, our pain is carried differently, if we can speak of it being carried at all. And the *why* disappears into the fact itself.

Why do we suffer?

Robert Aitken said: "Shakyamuni Buddha looked up and saw the morning star and exclaimed: 'I and all beings have at this moment attained the Way.' What did he realize?"

THE STORY OF Shakyamuni Buddha's awakening under the bodhi tree is the foundation myth of the Zen tradition, providing us with the deepest encouragement to awaken and confirm who we truly are—and always have been—and to walk the Way into our lives.

The Morning Star

We would normally, and properly, focus on Shakyamuni Buddha, but let's consider for a moment that intrepid star. Venus is the brightest object in our sky outside of the sun and the moon, and it is still visible in the dawn sky as the sun rises. At the breaking of dawn, she is the last star to disappear into its glory. In Western spiritual traditions Jesus is "the bright and morning star" and "a lamp shining in a dark place, until the day dawns and the morning star rises in our hearts."

Venus is both the morning star and the evening star:

the light and the dark, male and female, differentiation and emptiness, and their intimate interpenetration.

> In that moment of awakening, what did Shakyamuni Buddha realize? What was it that had him sweepingly exclaim that he and all beings—including you and me—in that instant had attained the Way?

CHARLOTTE JOKO BECK (1917–2011) was one of the
pioneer teachers in our Western tradition. Rather than
concentrating exclusively on traditional koan study,
she got her students to work with the issues that came
up in their lives. Because of this and her focus on
the psychological and the relational as central to Zen
practice generally, it was claimed that Joko was not
interested in enlightenment or even that she was not
enlightened. The following challenge, as recounted
in *The Hidden Lamp,* may have its roots in those
considerations:

> Joko Beck had just finished a talk and asked if
> there were any questions. A young man raised his
> hand and bluntly asked, "Are you enlightened?"
> Her response was immediate. Laughing she said,
> "I hope I should never have such a thought."

Joko's sparkling riposte gives the lie to all considerations of enlightenment or delusion—hers or others.
For Joko, enlightenment without meticulous character
development was as empty as practice without enlightenment. For her, character development and deepening of the Way through koan study needed to go hand
in hand.

Joko challenged her students hard, as in the following story by Paul Genki Kahn:

> During a difficult period of my life, everything seemed impossible. We were having beers together in a bar after a retreat in New York. I turned to Joko and cried out, "This shouldn't be happening to me." Joko responded instantly, "Exactly this should be happening to you." That is a teaching of a lifetime, a *nanto* koan.

With her koan "Don't be angry," Joko presents us with a challenge: how do we manifest our true and timeless nature when we are blocked by an unreasonable demand, especially one that impugns our authenticity and our rights? We don't want to be told what to do. We *should* be angry—at least about certain things.

The power of Joko's injunction is that it summons up the legacy of childhood: of being told what to do by our parents, teachers, and religious authorities—all that dictatorial weight of home, school, and the church. Joko's "Don't be angry" is also insidious, reminding me of those situations in relationships where one partner is about to offload some duplicity at which the other has every right to be furious. In these circumstances, "Don't be angry" is emotional blackmail. I can feel my anger rising as I write this.

On the other hand, we do need to restrain our anger. And we have to meet the challenge of this on a daily, if not hourly, basis in the workplace or in our relationships. We refrain from expressing our anger because anger hurts both others and ourselves. And if this is not too idealistic: anger is counterproductive for the good conduct of family, work, or our relationships generally; in fact unrestrained anger is mostly destructive across that range.

Sorrow, Fear, Anger

"Don't be angry" lands in our lives in complicated ways because our anger is so entangled with our fear and in measure with our sorrow. Sometimes we fear loss of control in a situation, so we use our anger to control or even to intimidate others, to keep them at bay. Or we may fear getting angry and losing it—and that very fear can become part of the buildup of more anger. "Losing it," reminds me of that vivid expression: "He was beside himself." When we lose it, we split from our own core and are accordingly ridiculous to others, even though they may be afraid of our rage.

With our anger we protect the softer more vulnerable parts of ourselves. We fear sorrow and loss; we fear losing out and the desolation that that brings; and so we become defensive, with anger as the chief means of our defense.

I'm not saying it is always wrong to be angry. But it is a shame to become an angry person. There is an old saying that the devil's crowning glory is an embittered old person. Think of embitterment as ossified anger; as in, she sits in the shadows arthritically revoking her will.

So Joko's blunt injunction "Don't be angry" carries

weight. However, "Don't be angry" is not solely concerned with controlling and modulating our anger; it is telling us that we shouldn't get angry at all—ever! This is where "Don't be angry" is at its most obnoxious, most outrageous . . .

Under the whip of "Don't be angry"—
what is your timeless essential nature?

INVESTIGATION 8: *The Moment of Pause*

We create the present moment through our attention to what is current. Thus we have the moment of breath, the moment of rage, the moment of chill.

The practice of Zen meditation over years widens the aperture of this moment. There are no shortcuts to this, and it unfolds out of reach of our conscious wishing and willing. With the widening aperture of this moment comes that pause before we react in provocative situations. The harm we might otherwise do to others and ourselves when we are driven about by our reactive impulses is thus reduced.

What do you experience in that moment of pause?

"Still wandering in your mind?" I asked Chris Barker.
"You bet," he responded.
"What's there?"
"Oh, gray sky, the sun on the salmon gums."

CHRIS BARKER and his partner, Jane Taylor, sat with the Zen Group of Western Australia in the later '90s. Chris and Jane were house managers at our Claremont Zendo, and their relative youth and the fact they were in love and in the early stages of a happy relationship that endures to this day warmed the Way for us. There was plenty of joie de vivre and a lot of good music happening in jams and impromptu performances between sesshins and weekly sits. Chris and Jane sat all the sesshins, were leaders, and supported the Sangha and myself.

"Still wandering in your mind?" I asked Chris. I expected to get his thoughts on art and reality, but I got the matter itself: *"Oh, gray sky, the sun on the salmon gums"* pointing to the profound nature of Mind—unnameable, timeless, weightless (though you still need to watch out when crossing the road!) as well as being without boundaries or dimension.

We might say that, on the one hand, there is the mind that thinks, reasons, fulminates, wonders, and complains, that we think of as being provisionally "inside our head," while on the other hand, we have Dogen's "Mind is mountains and rivers, the great earth itself, the sun, the moon, and the stars." Although these two "minds" may seem very different, there is not a breath between them.

Thoughts and Thinking

What we regard as "the mind inside the head" is characterized primarily by thinking—by what we often consider the bugbear of thinking. Yet, when we penetrate far enough into the nature of thoughts and thinking, we realize that even a single thought (sometimes so hard to locate in the thought-swarm)—"Oh, I forgot to pay the gas bill"—is itself the timeless place of no coming or going. Each thought, even the meanest, is thus. So although thoughts manifestly come and go, in their deepest nature they are no other than the place where coming or going is not even thought of.

Still wandering in your mind? What's there?

Realizing the Nature of Mind

I have given dokusan to several people who were dying, but Jane Taylor is the only person to whom I have given dokusan when she was breastfeeding. On this occasion, Jane was taking care of her first son, Nick. Was that dokusan for one or for two? Or three?

On another occasion, I asked Jane: "'Zen is the complete realization of mind'—what do you understand by that?" And she replied: "I can have silly thoughts." Jane's very words are the complete realization of mind, the complete cutting off of delusion. A silly thought is no less the Way than a profound one, as in the sublime nonsense of children's verse, such as Edward Lear's "The Owl and the Pussycat," which I'm teaching my grandchildren:

> The Owl and the Pussycat went to sea
> In a beautiful pea-green boat,
> They took some honey, and plenty of money,
> Wrapped up in a five-pound note.
>
> . . . .
>
> They dined on mince, and slices of quince,
> Which they ate with a runcible spoon;
> And hand in hand, on the edge of the sand,
> They danced by the light of the moon,
> The moon,
> The moon,
> They danced by the light of the moon.

To realize Mind, we don't seek truth, we don't avoid fantasy; sheerest nonsense conveys Mind unerringly, puffball light. Even derangement of the senses—if not of the mind—can do that. As the late-nineteenth-century French poet Arthur Rimbaud wrote in his *Une saison en enfer* (*A Season in Hell*): "I ended by considering my mind's disorder sacred." Even disordered consciousness is not other than Mind itself.

We have focused on thought as expressing the nature

of Mind, but my cat Possum conveys it just as well, as she inspects the sleeping guests.

Finally, nothing is left out, and the least regarded thing, or word—or even thought—is lit by the moon of enlightenment. What might have been formerly seen as a hindrance or something to be ignored, shines. This is the compendiousness; this is the generosity of the Zen Way, in which each of us—even with our lacks and limitations, even in our brokenness—includes the timeless expanse of the Way, while being accordingly included in it.

"Oh, gray sky, the sun on the salmon gums" is Mind in its vastness and purity: full of potential from which, *as which*, we all emerge. Mind is not something made up, remotely drifting at the edge of our consciousness. It is our birthright, timelessly established. We don't have to vainly try to jerry-build it; we are already it. And one hazy thought is enough to reveal that.

How do you convey the true nature of Mind?

INVESTIGATION 9: *The Story of Me*

What we call "the story of me" is made from our fleeting experiences and memories. We connect the dots, which is to say we marshal our scattered experiences and isolated memories and make up our narrative. Thus, with some radical editing, we concoct "the story of my life." We spend a lot of time polishing this story, bringing out the highlights and suppressing the painful bits, or dwelling on the painful humiliations and defending our right to feel aggrieved. But really we have nothing to defend.

Without your stories, who are you?

When he was in his eighties, my father was knocked
down by a delivery van. In hospital they put him in
"treatment," prior to admitting him as a patient.
Although no one could find time to get him a bottle
to piss in, four staff members came round with their
clipboards during the three hours he waited there,
to ask him his age. He generously gave each of them
a fresh response—"twenty-one," "ninety-eight,"
"forty-seven," and finally, "two hundred!"

MY FATHER came from the town of Walton-on-the-
Naze in Essex, England. He was a fine cricketer, a
champion swimmer (the cups he won sit on top of the
one ruined piano in my kitchen that faces westwards
towards the ocean), and although he had no musical
training, he could sing beautifully. I can remember him
singing both the melody and a harmony part of the old
song, "Forever and Ever." The lyrics convey my father:
a man of amiable spirit: faithful, loving, and one who
invariably lets bygones be bygones:

> Forever and ever my heart will be true.
> Sweetheart forever I'll wait for you.
> We both made a promise that we'd never part.
> Let's seal it with a kiss, forever my sweetheart.

Let bygones be bygones forever.
We'll fall in love once again.
So let's tell the world of our new love divine.
    Forever and forever you'll be mine.

These English lyrics were written by Malia Rosa in 1948 to the music of a German song, "Fliege mit mir in die Heimat" (Fly with Me in the Homeland) written by the Austrian songwriter Franz Winkler.

My father came to Western Australia in the 1930s and survived the Great Depression by working at a variety of jobs including house painter, roof plumber, and hospital orderly. It was in the last capacity that he met my mother in the laundry of the King Edward Memorial Hospital, the maternity hospital where, many years later, my children were born.

When my father briefly returned to England in the mid-1960s, he learned that he had Austrian forebears, including an Austrian baron, no less. I was delighted, having been immersed for a time in the music of Mozart, Beethoven, and Schubert—the First Viennese School— and beginning to discover the composers of the second: Schoenberg, Berg, and Webern. I also learned from my father that his father had been a dealer in books, buying up libraries in Prussia, Austria-Hungary, and Russia. He then started a bookshop in London to sell those collections.

During my growing up, my father worked at Metters, an ancient stove factory that shed rusting iron onto the hill overlooking our home. It was a vast echoing space, completely dark except for an occasional dim unshielded electric light. My father sweated in summer, froze in winter, and, due to the unrelieved industrial noise, went slowly deaf. I remember with gratitude how hard my mother and father worked to ensure I got an education.

My father had endless problems with his hearing aids, and the accident described above occurred after I had taken him to visit the audiologist. Afterwards, for the first time ever, my father suggested that we should have a coffee, so with him shuffling and tottering, we headed out across St. George's Terrace towards the Mocha Coffee House, my arm in his tweedy arm. For one dark instant I looked down at his uncertain feet. Then I was lying on him, pinning him to the road. There was blood on his hand. The white panel van that had hit us looked huge from below. A businessman came with water and offered to phone "my office" on his mobile. The face of the teenage van driver appeared for a moment, pasty and terrified. I felt such gratitude to them all, as my father and I lay helplessly in the road.

In hospital they put him in "treatment," prior to admitting him as a patient. As there was no one in charge, I broke regulations to keep him company. Sitting up in bed, his gray hair swept up onto the high white pillow and his nose beaked commandingly, he looked like a distinguished conductor. Although no one could find time to get him a bottle to piss in, four staff members came round with their clipboards during the three hours he waited, to ask him his age. He generously gave each of them a fresh response—"twenty-one," "ninety-eight," "forty-seven," and finally, "two hundred!"

As a gauge of maturity on the Way, I would include grace under pressure: that ability to deal lightly and freely with what is difficult, to find the freedom and the grace to play, even in our pain and distress. My father, while not a Zen practitioner in the formal sense, exemplifies this most aptly for me. When I was going to Hawaii to do my first Zen Training Period with Robert Aitken, as a way of trying to help my parents make sense of a quest that they must have regarded as the pinnacle of religious lunacy, I gave them a copy of Aitken's book *Taking the Path of Zen* to read. When he handed it back to me several weeks later, my father said: "It's okay, but there's a bit too much church." Later he said: "I wish you everything you wish yourself."

In Zen we are not attached to name or form, nor are we attached to number. Our true nature is timeless. As one of my students put it regarding herself: "I am as old as the night sky."

How can you find your own true and timeless nature in my father's joking responses to the ward staff?

Father and Son Zen 16

When my son was in his early teens he asked me,
"What is Zen, Dad?"
"Well, it's like when you're out sailing
and you are one with your yacht," I said.
"That sounds like when I'm having a good sail, Dad."
"And that's it too," I replied.

MY SON JULIAN and my daughter Amanda both grew up exposed to Zen teachers and students, which I think for the most part was a low-key orientation to the Way. Glenys, my wife in that time, and I were clear that we didn't want Amanda and Julian brought up in any kind of formal religion, and we were strong on not inflicting religious forms on them. I had seen children being initiated into the forms of Thich Nhat Hanh–style Vietnamese Zen: pouring tea on the baby Buddha, learning how to *gassho* and to bow, but I felt uncomfortable about the prospect of teaching these forms to my children. The nearest we got to a Zen religious form was holding hands silently for a few moments before beginning a meal, and I used to joke that it was only to avert the "bog-in-don't-wait" stampede.

I think the hour I spent meditating each morning was a mystery to my children, and I wish I had been more forthcoming about what I was doing. Glenys would explain to them: "Daddy's sort of praying."

It seemed to me that the main thing was to respond to any questions they brought up and to leave it at that. I remember sitting up in the spreading branches of a tree in our backyard with Julian and him asking: "Is God in trees?" I said "yes" (although I am not drawn to pantheism), which initiated an interesting discussion about God being in everything.

When he was in his early teens, Julian became passionate about sailing Moths. A "Moth" is the name for a small development class of sailing dinghy. We would strap Julian's Moth to the roof rack of my car and head to the river—at the risk of being pulled over by the police because the Moth would be protrude over both ends of the car. Julian became an excellent Moth sailor and won many races.

One day, Julian asked me "What is Zen?" and the straightforwardness of his question took my breath away. Nevertheless I stammered out, "Well, it's like when you're out sailing and you are one with your yacht."

We get rather sniffy about "oneness" in Zen, lining it up with the old hippie's "It's all one, man," which is meant to function as a panacea for any conceivable form of human suffering from the disasters of war to a disagreement about the fence that separates neighbors. We call the hippie position "pernicious oneness"—a lazy account of reality, usually without any experiential base. The best thing going for pernicious oneness is the joke: A hippie orders a hamburger, telling the stall owner, "Make me one with everything."

But under the duress of my son's challenging question, I reached for what was nearest: "Well, it's like when you're out sailing and you are one with your yacht." Julian came back with: "That sounds like when I'm having a good sail, Dad." Firmly based in his experience, Julian's words perfectly express the Way. And with my "And that's it too," I happily confirm his words with my own.

What is the essence of true Dharma in this story?

How would you explain Zen to a teenager?

Rainer Maria Rilke's "Our Inner Seasons" 17

How we squander our hours of pain.
How we gaze beyond them into the bitter duration
to see if they have an end. Though they are really
seasons of us, our winter-enduring foliage, ponds,
meadows, our inborn landscape, where birds
and reed-dwelling creatures are at home.
—RAINER MARIA RILKE

THE BOHEMIAN-AUSTRIAN POET Rainer Maria Rilke (1875–1926) is widely regarded as one of the greatest German poets, in company with Goethe and Hölderlin. Writing in both German and French, he is a transitional figure between the late romantic poets and the modernists. Rilke's Duino Elegies were completed in 1922 and are the summit of his poetic output. At times dazzlingly obscure, they express themes of existential suffering and alienation, but also at points they evoke a reality that yearns for us to accord with it, and to give it expression. Responding to this summons is the poet's mission, but it is also for Rilke our task and mission. All this connects strongly with the Zen Way and may have had as its source Rilke's awakening experience in 1907 or 1908 while he was staying on Capri.

There are now more than twenty translations of the Duino Elegies into English. This is indicative of how popular these challenging works have become in the English-speaking world, especially in the United States, where Rilke is seen as a spiritual guide. Quotes from his work turn up frequently in New Age literature: profound images of no-self in the self-help section of the bookshop.

Suffering and Our Attempts to Escape It

We are geared to avoid suffering, so it is small wonder we find it challenging to allow it. Understandably, we wonder when will this suffering end? Knowing that even harsh pain will pass may give us hope, but the visceral realities are powerful and difficult to ignore. And if we can't evade them, what do we do?

When we attempt to flee it, pain drags us back and becomes all the more acute because it is driven by our fear. This is true for emotional as well as physical pain. No wonder we try to gaze beyond such pain to see if it has an end; yet this evasion squanders our opportunity to allow, to attend, and to become intimate with our hours of pain—which are really, as Rilke puts it, "seasons of us." In a culture of distraction, we become adept at diverting ourselves or allowing ourselves to be sidetracked to the point that it can be difficult to find the private time and space to attend at all. We lose connection—with the seasons, with ourselves, and with each other. In his First Duino Elegy Rilke writes:

> Yes—the spring times needed you. Often a star
> was waiting for you to notice it. A wave rolled
>   toward you

out of the distant past, or as you walked
under an open window, a violin
yielded itself to your hearing. All this was
   mission. But could you accomplish it?
   Weren't you always
distracted by expectation, as if every event
announced a beloved?

Our "mission" is to accord with reality and to give
it expression. In the deepest sense, the springtime not
only needs you, it is no other than you, yourself; likewise the star, the wave, and the violinist practicing the
Bach Chaconne in the attic.

Rilke saw our task as being here for what is, for
what calls to us, often so unavailingly. This is the poet's
mission, and it is also the mission for us all. Each day
offers itself, unconcerned that we're so little there for it.
But the glory is not elsewhere. Far beyond the magical
thinking of romantic love, each moment, each event, is
presenting our beloved, and it does this unfailingly. In
this spirit, who or what is your beloved?

Rilke's Experience on Capri

I believe that Rilke's Duino Elegies—especially the
ninth and the fragmentary early version of what became
the tenth from which our current koan is taken—were
shaped by an experience of seeing into his true nature
(kensho) when he was staying on Capri in 1907 or
1908. Rilke, referring to himself in the third person,
recounts his experience as follows:

He recalled the hour spent in that other garden of the South (Capri) when a bird-call sounded simultaneously outside and within himself. The bird-call seemed not to be refracted on the barrier of his body, but to collect both spheres together into one continuous space, where there remained, mysteriously protected, only one spot of purest and most profound consciousness. On this occasion he closed his eyes, so as not to be distracted amid such a magnificent experience by the contour of his own body; the infinite passed into him from all sides so intimately that he imagined that he felt the gentle presence of the stars which had settled in his breast.

Rilke's experience—provoked by the bird call—is one of unbidden intimacy: an intimacy that does not know its own source. To have such an experience is not to lose our self in the purity of the void; rather the infinite finds its home within us, as us. From this concurrence—evoked by Rilke as "the gentle presence of the stars which had settled in his breast"—arise the inner seasons and the inborn landscape that is home to reed-dwelling creatures, and indeed to all beings. This is our innermost reality, our true and timeless nature.

We will now proceed to explore these inner seasons and their significance for traveling the Zen Way.

Our Inner Seasons

Those hours of pain we squander are our inner seasons, and predictably Rilke locates those interminable hours in winter, and those hours of pain, grief, and loss are, as he puts it, our "winter-enduring foliage"—the pain that holds us and indeed is us. Finding hard-won ease and release by becoming intimate with those hours of loss, despair, and remorse is our Way. In the light of this, I ask you: "What is your best season?"

Rilke's line, "our inborn landscape, where birds and reed-dwelling creatures are at home," introduces us to that innerness that is our birthright. Timeless and infinite, it readily includes those reed-dwelling creatures—ducks, geese, swans, grebes, pelicans, cormorants, ibis, egrets, herons—as well as frogs and platypuses, freshwater turtles, water dragons and snakes, as well as us and all our mammalian companions, to boot.

Compassion Arises from Intimacy with Our Own Pain

We become intimate with those hours of pain as they unfold. With this we become more available and more open. We notice this in our dealings with others. Often, when we are happy or at least pleased with ourselves, we aren't there for others at all. Their needs bounce off our hard surfaces. Contrariwise, when we are sad, our heart is often more open for others, and we find ourselves more available: giving their car a push when their battery is flat, or minding their kids when they are having an emergency.

In his image of our "inborn landscape," Rilke speaks for the warmth, inclusiveness, and compassion of the heart, which opens when we are willing to be with our own suffering. Creatures—no less than other human beings—make a beeline for such love. Rilke speaks for this, surely, but he also speaks for something more.

What is your inborn landscape?

INVESTIGATION 10: *The Time of Your Life*

I love the expression "the time of your life," with its sense of celebration as when we say, "You're having the time of your life." As I write this, I'm celebrating my seventieth birthday—the biblical three-score-and-ten—and in the midst of the troubles that come with any long tenure on the earth, I'm having the time of my life. But what is the time of our life, more ordinarily? A long time? A short time? How long does your life feel?

We know that time is fleeting, and we feel the arrow of time in our aging, ailing bodies; but life can still feel long with its weight of years or because it has become wearisome or because it is so loaded with experience that is rich and consequential for us. How much we remember and the intensity of that remembering may also influence our perception of the length of our life.

The length of our life, in felt rather than chrono-logical terms, seems mysterious. The question, "What is the length of my life?" is rather like the question, "What was the length of my dream?" Both are perhaps equally undecidable.

It is possible that looking back just as we are about to die, our life will seem short, maybe just a rapid flashback of memories. From your present perspective though, what is the length of your life? This investigation becomes more koan-like if you pose this consideration against Joko Beck's, "Nothing has ever existed except this moment. That's all there is. That's all we are."

How long is your life?

Issan Dorsey's "You Get What You Deserve Whether You Deserve It or Not" 18

ISSAN DORSEY was born Tommy Dorsey Jr. in 1933 in Santa Barbara, California. He was raised in a Catholic family, the youngest of ten siblings. As a boy he aspired to become an entertainer and studied dance and piano. While in junior college he became dissatisfied with his life, so he joined the U.S. Navy. During the Korean War, Dorsey and a male lover were expelled from the Navy, giving him the opportunity to spend several years in and out of employment, finally settling into a job as a waiter in a bar in North Beach and becoming a performer there. As a drag queen, Tommy Dee—"who looked like the girl next door"—worked the bars, dealt drugs, did cabaret, and worked as a male prostitute.

Tommy underwent a transformation in the late 1960s when he began sitting with Shunryu Suzuki (1904–1971) at the San Francisco Zen Center. Walking down Haight Street one day he stooped to pick up a candy wrapper.

I bent down and picked it up, and right as I did, I said to myself, "Does this mean I am responsible for everything I see?" I told myself it didn't, but actually I knew that it did.

Tommy was eventually ordained by Richard Baker, Suzuki's successor and abbot of the San Francisco Zen Center, and given the Dharma name Issan. What emerges from Issan's long commitment to the San Francisco Zen Center is his humanity: his unassuming kindness, humor, and the depth of his involvement. Dharma became his life and the Sangha his long-sought family. This was evident in the crisis that engulfed the Zen Center when Baker was found to be having an extramarital affair with the wife of one of the Sangha's benefactors and was forced to resign. Issan stayed loyal to Baker throughout. When he was questioned about this, he simply said, "But he's my teacher."

In his final years Dorsey served a gay community blighted by AIDS. In 1987 he created Maitri Hospice within the Zen Center on Hartford Street, primarily caring for gay men who were dying of AIDS. There's a humorous, even mythic, story from this period of his life, that I particularly love:

One bright afternoon, Issan was walking down Hartford St. towards 18th with Steve Allen and Jerry Berg. Steve and Jerry were talking about possible legal structures for the hospice while Issan lagged behind. He noticed a bottle lying on the sidewalk and bent to pick it up. The bottle was rather beautiful, so he took out the rag that he kept neatly folded in his monk's handbag, and began to polish it. Suddenly, a genie appeared! It had to be a Buddhist genie, a Bodhidharma look-a-like, with a shaved head, droopy ears and a bright robe. The genie looked at Issan and Issan looked back. Steve and Jerry turned around to see what was holding Issan up and stopped dead in their tracks.

The genie spoke the time honored script of genies: "Because you have freed me after many lifetimes of being cramped-up in that god damned bottle, you, yeah, I guess all three of you, get one wish. It's just one so you'd better make it good."

Steve didn't hesitate: he asked to be released from his karma and enter Nirvana. As he was about to raise his palms in gassho—poof, he was gone.

Jerry thought to himself, that was powerful magic. I'm going for it. I'm not getting any younger so how about a great life in a heaven modeled after Palm Springs—but without the humidity— endless pool parties, rafts of handsome men, an eternal nosh that never made you fat? As he smiled and waved good-bye—poof, he disappeared too.

The genie turned to Issan who was left standing alone. The genie said, "OK, honey, it's your turn, what does your little heart desire?"

Issan didn't hesitate, "Get those two numb-nut girls back here. We have a hospice to run."

What is the essence of true Dharma in this story?

Issan contracted HIV himself, suffering a long, painful illness before his death in 1990. He was fifty-seven years old.

You Get What You Deserve
Whether You Deserve It or Not

It's great to have a koan so focused on karma. Surely Issan understood karmic consequence because he lived life at levels of intensity and risk that few of us could, or might even indeed wish to. Issan's koan gives the nod to karma in its rawest most retributive sense—"You get what you deserve . . ." You do someone a bad turn, and you get your comeuppance. Or you do someone a good turn, and consequently feel that you deserve acknowledgment. This is all about "getting what you deserve." But what about "whether you deserve it or not"?

What is it to get what you don't deserve?

Concerning Karma

In the popular imagination, karma is chiefly seen as retributive. This is because we are bound up in the dramas the small self. However, personal retribution and reward are only a tiny part of the karmic drama.

The overwhelming karmic fact of life is that we are born at all, and that we are born into this universe that is some 13.8 billion years old, on this strange and beautiful planet, which we humans are so busy despoiling. How strange, how miraculous. Our karma is also intensely bound up in whether we are born male or female. Our gender determines a lot about who we are, though it's not immutable, as transsexuality shows. Our genetic inheritance is important too, and on a vaster scale—going all the way back to the single-celled amoeba—our evolutionary inheritance. Obviously the culture into which we are born and the country in which we are raised have karmic outcomes for us. We inhabit the reality of our inherited situation, especially our biological inheritance, whether we like it or not, whether we deserve it or not.

We don't have to deserve our life, it's freely given. Our life unfolds beyond being deserved or not being deserved. Our heart beats, our blood circulates, whether we deserve it or not; we are born regardless of our deserving, we grow up and mature regardless, we get our heart broken regardless, and we die regardless of whether we deserve it or not.

All these larger karmic forces play out beyond simple retributive karma, which is the part we are mostly interested in. We take the big karmic picture for granted, but it's good to bring it into focus. Although it is true that our past actions often generate present consequences, and we can ruefully acknowledge that we got what we deserved, I doubt that this sliver of retributive karma is in any way absolute. It is certainly easy to imagine it otherwise, and I suspect it often is. To take retributive karma as absolute is to take an awful lot on trust.

We conventionally regard karma as cause and effect unfolding in a linear way: this leads to that, which leads to this, and so on. But we can also understand karma as mysterious affinity, especially as it finds its expression through love, but also friendships, family, and Sangha relations. Mysterious affinity—essentially clusterings that elude explanation in terms of cause and effect—can powerfully shape our life.

The Accord of Karmic and Essential

Yet finally the karmic and the essential—which is to say the realm of the timelessly empty—are no other than one another. They waltz themselves into union and out again—all the while being inseparable. Here's a story—really a koan—involving Issan that bears witness to this:

> Issan had contracted AIDS and was very weak and close to death. A friend of his was carrying him to the toilet. Looking down at Issan and seeing how pitifully emaciated he looked, his friend burst into tears, and said, "I'll miss you Issan." Issan replied, "I'll miss you too—are you going away?"

Leaning on Karma; Leaning on the Essential

When we pit the karmic against the essential, it is like riding a horse and falling off on one side or the other. The karmic extreme, where you fall off on the left side, might go like this: "Well, I can't help my upbringing. My parents' marriage was so awful, what hope is there for mine?" As further support for falling into karmic extremity, I remember a Danish man called Bjorn, who lived opposite me for many years and built a formidable brick house over the old wooden house that had for-

merly been rented by alternative folk who played gui-
tar and smoked a lot of dope on their front veranda.
Whatever Bjorn was telling me about his life, he always
added resignedly, "You get that," as in "My son refuses
to do his homework—you get that."

Bjorn had worked as a radio operator for the U.S.
military in Greenland. He told me: "I would have radio
contact with pilots flying at night. Then radio contact
would cease, and you knew that their plane had flown
into the side of a mountain in the darkness. You get
that." Such numb fatalism is a good gauge of someone
falling off at the karmic extremity.

Back to the horse: When you fall off on the right
side, the essential side, it's like: "Well, no need to worry
about any of those issues; it's all one, buddy." This
is pernicious oneness. Good to avoid falling into that
also. Our only job, under constant threat of falling
off left or right, is to stay in the saddle, and the saddle
turns out to be remarkably large.

**You get what you deserve. You get what you get.
You are what you get. You get what you are. You get
that? What is it to get what you deserve whether you
deserve it or not?**

INVESTIGATION 11: *Only Just This*

As we mature in the Way, we come to live the timeless moment as our true face and being. Past and future are ever-changing expressions flitting over it. We lose ourselves as we become intimate with remembering and planning, in walking out in the spring sun. Everything is passing away, just as we ourselves are. Yet when we become intimate with the timelessness of where and when, we are in contact with the whole and are not other than it. In the same breath, we are very small, limited, and mortal. In this spirit we don't regard each moment as an epiphany. Why should the moment be so privileged; why should we be so privileged? Rather we just attend to what is, to what needs doing—the ordinary miracle of that—and the rest looks after itself, or fails to.

I remember mentioning a student's experience of seeing a blue light in her meditation to John Tarrant. We were crossing an intersection in Perth, and John responded: "Well, I think the green light is a good deal more important than the blue light."

No need to summon up the extraordinary. In the whole vast universe, there is this: just this. Just this early summer heat, just this tiredness, just the wind scattering jacaranda blossoms out across the hot road.

**In your unrepeatable moment of right now,
who are you?**

Anne Carson's "There Is No Person without a World" 19

OUR LIVES belong to us, of course they do. Or do they? There are so many participants who have a stake in our lives, that our ownership may not be so clear after all. Well, "If not my life, then whose?" you might ask. Yet, although our lives are personal, they are also in common, and fundamentally, not really owned at all.

We might be inclined to say: "It's my life, and I'll do what I want with it." Of course. Yet if, for example, we commit suicide, the impact on our family will be incalculable. What we do with "our lives" really matters. It bears on others. We can destroy others when we destroy our own lives.

The Dharma is the law of the universe, a law that may be expressed simply as: *One thing depends upon another. I am because you are; you are because I am.* Each one of us is like this in our relation to others, and indeed to the world.

When we realize that the world is not just some painted backdrop to our fantasies of power and control, but our true face and home we realize the deep sense of this line by Canadian poet Anne Carson: "There is no person without a world."

In one of Buddhism's iconic images, Gautama Buddha sits in meditation with his left palm facing upwards in his lap, while his right hand touches the earth.

During his long sojourn under the bodhi tree before his great enlightenment, demonic forces tried to unseat him because their king Mara claimed that place under the bodhi tree. Mara demanded that Gautama produce a witness to confirm his spiritual awakening. The Buddha simply touched the earth with his right hand. Traditional accounts have the earth literally speaking on behalf of the Buddha, saying—or rather roaring—"I am your witness!" However, there are more subtle ways the earth bears witness on our behalf. Can you present one?

Listen. Listen.

The Buddha's gesture of touching the earth and calling it to bear witness shows the indissoluble connection that each of us has to the earth and discloses our true and timeless nature. When we realize who we truly are, and our dependence on all that is, we also comprehend that we have responsibilities to the world and to each other.

Bearing Witness: Fire-Stick Farming

There is no person without a world. If the world perishes, we perish. If we are going to survive and ensure the survival of other species, we must bear witness to them by maintaining the earth and by caring for it. The most exemplary form of this care that I know is the Aboriginal practice of fire-stick farming and land management, a practice that goes back for time immemorial. Bill Gammage in his classic book *The Biggest Estate on Earth* writes that Aboriginal people created an extraordinarily complex system of land management using fire and the life cycles of native plants to ensure plentiful wildlife and plant foods throughout the year. Their practice of fire-stick farming is about how to burn well; it's about how to use fire discretely and how to prevent the gigantic and destructive fires that will likely multiply as we advance further into global warming.

The practice of fire-stick farming is exemplary in how it treats the earth and sentient beings. It shows us how it is possible to take care of our environment while shaping it so that not only humans can thrive, but also all life. I recently heard a radio program about a "cool burn" in and around Orange in southern New South Wales. Aboriginal people were doing the cool burn in order to prevent massively destructive bush-fires. I was especially moved by the mention of the fact that cool burning is *slow burning*, and that slow burning gives animals and insects time to escape, to get out of the way. Cool burning also means that you burn in a mosaic and, hence, don't burn everything. For example, you don't burn out the home range—say twenty-five acres—of a bird; otherwise the bird has nothing to eat. The fires are cool enough for families to walk through. Moisture on the ground protects invertebrates. Flames don't go up into the canopy, which means the fire doesn't spread out of control. By burning the undergrowth you reduce the chance of the out-of-control conflagrations we know today, as climate change advances into its more destructive phases.

Engagement is key in cool burning. In effecting it you are caring for country. One of the old Aboriginal men on the program said: "You look after country, country look after you." And it was also said that by looking after country, you are also caring for your community. It is hard to imagine a better illustration of how to live mutual interdependency, how to live *there is no person without a world*.

How do you live "There is no person without a world"?

How Do You Find True Freedom at Work? 20

THE NOBILITY OF manual labor is surely an aristocratic notion. From a worker's perspective, a lot of work isn't fit for humans to do, for work isn't thoughtfully divided up on the basis of job satisfaction by those who organize it; rather it is organized so as to maximize profit and for the most efficient use of available resources, including the human ones. If it weren't for the fact that they had to feed a family or pay off a mortgage, many people wouldn't work at all. My neighbor tells me: "My cat doesn't work. I want to come back as a cat."

The notion that work should be meaningful—in addition to being necessary to feed mouths and pay bills—is of recent origin and an idea that has probably exacerbated the problem of work for many people. Yet in many instances just having a job—or two or three if we are moonlighting—is a blessing because the financial and personal perils of unemployment impact savagely on those who depend on us, as well as on ourselves.

I remember that fifty years ago, many people were optimistic that robots and computers would free us all from soul-destroying work and create extensive leisure. But the current reality is that many people work harder, if they haven't actually lost their jobs due to outsourcing, automation, or an app. Many people derive an

uncertain income from part-time or short-term employment, without the benefits of guaranteed hours, income
security, and the right to adequate workplace health
and safety. As a musician, I remember describing a
recent Australian economic downturn to my producer
and friend Anthony Cormican, who laughed and said,
"Economic downturn? That's where we live!"

If we get to work at all, work will be where we spend
a lot of our time. Bringing up children, paying off a
mortgage, or needing the basic necessities of life to survive means that we probably don't have much choice
about having to work either. So how do we find freedom where our choices are much diminished and where
inevitably we have to engage with people we don't like
and who don't like us?

When we find true freedom, we are liberated from
the burden of our separated self with its blinkered
view of reality conditioned by its need to be in control.
To find true freedom is to find intimacy with what is
current, rather than darting about everywhere in the
pursuit of a happiness that tends to be elusive, most
especially when we pursue it.

**How do you find true freedom in the challenging cir-
cumstances of your workplace?**

Nick Arnold's "What Is the True Value of Your Money?" 21

NICK ARNOLD is the treasurer for the Zen Group of Western Australia. Through his leadership, devotion to the Way, and very considerable IT skills, he has helped to bring our group into the twenty-first century, as well as consolidating and streamlining its financial base as treasurer.

Nick was driving me to a council meeting, and I took the opportunity to ask him what he thought would be a good money koan. We discussed this for a time, and Nick finally said: "What is the true value of your money?"—a fine koan indeed.

We live in societies that place a high, even inordinate value on money and whatever it can purchase. It's true that not having enough money to purchase food and shelter can range from problematic to desperate. On the other hand, having a lot of money, or at least far more than we need, tends to bring more cares and responsibilities, rather than freeing us from them. Nick drew my attention to the fact that the relentless pursuit of wealth and power gives weight to the saying: "He who dies with the most toys wins."

How much is enough? I think that when our basic needs and the basic needs of those who rely on us are met, we don't need a lot more to lead a satisfying life.

I have been a musician since I was fifteen. My

professional career began with me asking the rich folks ("the upper-ups," as my mother termed them) on the Western hill for five pounds when they invited me to play accordion for their barbecue. Five pounds earned me the freedom to conduct the girl I was in love with to the school ball by taxi, rather than have my parents drive us. This is a perfect example of how money can buy freedom—but not love.

Years later, I played piano at the Hilton: five years in the salubrious and cripplingly expensive Garden Restaurant, then a year playing solo piano in the front bar to pay off a chunk of a mortgage and to help support my family. It hasn't been a career from which I expected to become wealthy, but the opportunity to play and compose—the latter mostly on my own terms—has been gratifying.

Given that we can't take it with us, what is the true value of our money? We conventionally think of this as its purchasing power: AU$10 will buy you a coffee and a croissant in an average Perth café or a cheap edition of Tolstoy's *Anna Karenina*; it will buy you a mediocre cocktail or a homeless person a basic meal of curry and rice and a pakora at Govinda's, the local Hare Krishna restaurant. But what is the true and genuine value of AU$10?

Giving and Receiving

We've been focused on getting, but what about giving, and in particular, giving money? Meister Eckhart wrote: "To give a thousand Marks of gold to build a church or a cloister would be a great thing, but to give a thousand Marks for nothing at all would be a far greater gift."

Gratitude is implicit in giving for its own sake: gratitude for the opportunity to give, gratitude for being one among the many who can contribute to the building of a Sangha, gratitude to be able to participate in turning the Dharma wheel.

Even meditation itself feels like an act of undirected gratitude: gratitude without expectation of reward. We meditate for its own sake. In this regard, Zen isn't instrumental, which is to say, it isn't concerned with the creation of particular states, such as relaxation or bliss, though these tend to occur as by-products of practice. And it isn't about self-improvement, or getting on in the world, although sustained practice may help us to stay steady in challenging situations. Again that is not the purpose of the Way. We practice for its own sake. Our life is for its own sake. What are we here for? Is there a purpose for us being here? When love and work are going well, we may feel as if that is why we are here, and we are inclined to say that our life has purpose and meaning. However, the Way cuts deeper than meaning in life. We are no other than life—not just our own life—in its unfolding.

Who Benefits from Your Generosity?

In *The Hidden Lamp: Stories from Twenty-Five Centuries of Awakened Women,* Amy Hollowell has this beautiful koan: "Who benefits from your generosity?"

To be clear, this isn't about making a list of the charities that you support—not at all, although we surely hope that people will benefit from our donations.

Correspondingly, the question "What is the true value of your money?" is not concerned, at depth, with the purchasing power of your dollar. True value is beyond the relativities of gain and loss, wealth and poverty.

My friend Martin Seddon and I joke about being retired to the park bench to talk philosophy and to read Proust. Martin celebrated his sixty-fifth birthday recently, and on his way back to the car with his wife and family, they came across a homeless man begging. Martin said, "I thought to give him $5, but I offered him $50 instead and gave myself a happy birthday."

What is the true value of your money?

When you are at a party that is very loud and distracting,
just close your eyes for a moment,
and you'll find your treasure is right there.
At such a time, what is your treasure?
—NYOGEN SENZAKI

NYOGEN SENZAKI (1876–1958) was the first major
Zen teacher to reside in the United States. Not much
is known about his early years, but the story goes that
Senzaki's mother was Japanese, his father either Chinese or Russian, and Senzaki was born and orphaned
in Siberia, where a passing Japanese monk had found
him lying next to his mother's frozen body. He was
adopted by a shipwright named Senzaki and came
under the care of a Soto Zen priest and Kegon Buddhist
scholar who began teaching him the Chinese classics,
along with Buddhism. By the age of eighteen Senzaki
had read the entire Chinese Tripitaka. He was ordained
as an *unsui* in the Soto sect and given the name "Nyogen," which means in Japanese "Like a dream, like a
fantasy"—an image that has its source in the concluding lines of the Diamond Sutra:

All things are under the law of change. They are

a dream, a phantom, a bubble, or a shadow. They are like dew or a flash of lightning . . .

In 1896 Nyogen went to Engakuji and became the Rinzai master Soyen Shaku's student, traveling with him to the United States in 1905. Soyen Shaku (1860–1919) taught Ida and Alexander Russell and their family at their home outside of San Francisco, while Senzaki was Soyen's attendant, as well as being houseboy. There is a great story from that time (as told by Rick Fields):

After Senzaki had been sacked as houseboy, that same evening Soyen [Shaku] accompanied Senzaki on his way to a Japanese hotel in San Francisco. They were walking through Golden Gate Park when Soyen stopped, set down Senzaki's suitcase, which he had been carrying, and said, "This may be better for you instead of being hampered as my attendant monk. Just face the great city and see whether it conquers you or you conquer it." Then he turned quickly away, said goodbye and disappeared into the evening fog. It was the last time Senzaki ever saw him.

What a way to be thrown in at the deep end! It is said that Nyogen Senzaki read every book on Buddhism in the San Francisco Public Library. Then, in 1922, he hired a hall and gave his first lecture on Zen. Thus began his "floating zendo" in which he led the itinerant groups that gathered around him over the next thirty years.

At the conclusion of the war Senzaki moved his

"floating zendo" to Los Angeles. While making his living in a number of ways, he devoted his passion for the rest of his life to teaching Zen. Among his students was Robert Aitken, who would become one of the most important Western Zen teachers. Nyogen Senzaki taught and inspired many others who helped to establish the Zen Way in the United States. He was a great pioneer who kept his monk's vows and lived simply, so much so that his students found it hard to offer him support. One strategy they devised was to leave a five-dollar bill in the zendo bell. When Senzaki discovered the money, he would immediately invite any student who happened to be around to accompany him to have a meal at a nearby restaurant. Senzaki may have been poor, but he liked to have a good time—which brings us neatly to his koan about being at a raucous party.

What Is Your Treasure?

To ask about your treasure is to enquire about your true nature. In this instance the question concerns who you truly are when you are at a loud and distracting party. The Zen Way is not just sitting on your cushion; you must be able to live the Way in all the phases and aspects of your life, including celebrations. Zen people are often more at home in a crisis—for instance helping people who are facing death—than they are at a celebration. So, in the light of this, a noisy party is a challenge to a student of the Way that shouldn't be shirked.

Because Senzaki formulates his koan in terms of a raucous party, I will take the opportunity to introduce the koan "Who is hearing that sound?" to help us uncover a path to the treasure of who we truly are.

"Who is hearing that sound?" is not a Western koan; it comes down to us from the fourteenth-century Japanese Zen master Bassui Tokusho (1327–1387). The koan as he devised it was: "Who is the Master of hearing that sound?"

"Who is hearing that sound?"—or its shorter form, "Who hears?"—has some currency in the West these days, and I have found it efficacious as a first barrier koan. "Who hears?" is also easy to carry into everyday life situations, enabling us to sustain the questioning there. After all, we are, like it or not, in an ocean of sounds, any of which can initiate our questioning as to the one who hears.

The Buddha is said to have told Avalokiteshvara that there are eighteen great gates to the Way, and that the first of these is sound. Sound is a Dharma gate—a point of entry into the Way, and often the first one for students. Accordingly, sound is important— even fundamental—to Zen practice. We ask, "Who is hearing that sound?" rather than "Who is seeing?" although the latter is also a viable koan. When we do zazen, our eyes are open just a little ("a hooded gaze") so that the visual realm is diminished, and the subtle realm of sound swims up.

Sounds are unbounded, and each or any of them can toll the death knell for our small limited self.

How to Practice with the Koan "Who Hears?"

When you become aware of a sound, or when a sound impinges, simply ask, "Who hears?" In terms of working with "Who hears?" it is good to let go of notions like "inside sounds" and "outside sounds." The sound of you cleaning your teeth or your tummy rumbling before a meal or even the sound of your heart beating if you can hear it is grist for your investigation, along with the rumble of distant traffic or the sound of your neighbor flushing the toilet. There is no need to scour the horizon for sounds when it's quiet, either. Just ask the question, and there is your sound.

Each sound brings you home; each sound is home. It's good not to name the sounds or to get carried away with their associations either, as when you hear the sound of rain starting up and you remember that there's a leak in your roof and that you will need to ring the plumber and that last time you did that it took a week before he was able to get out to fix that leak . . . That kind of thinking can pull you off course forever—just *drip! drip! drip!* Who is hearing that? If the response comes, "I am hearing"—which is true in its way— you then just ask, "Who is that one? Who is that 'I' that hears?" Thus you begin your journey. Whatever arises by way of a response—"Everyone is hearing that sound" or "No one is hearing that sound"—just let those conceptions go and continue to ask, "Who hears?"

When we meditate with "Who is hearing that sound?" the dark region is the question as to *who* is hearing. *Who* is the one who hears? It is helpful to cue "Who hears?" or even more succinctly, "Who?" to your breath. This helps to disperse thought and enables you to settle more readily into the koan. When you ask, on hearing a sound, "Who hears?" or "Who?" you raise your enquiring spirit—absolutely vital for your quest.

Your journey with "Who hears?" takes you beneath your name and roles. Your roles and socially constructed notions of who you are may be powerfully established; however, as you deepen in to the koan, and it becomes intimate with you, those conceptions begin to release their grip.

Eventually you reach a place where you are blocked, where you have run out of conceptual resources, and you truly don't know who hears. In that place just continue to ask "Who hears?" and deepen the question tirelessly to the extreme. You don't need a placid, deep place free of thoughts and thinking to realize either. You may be besieged with thoughts or overcome by emotion or be completely unable to deal with Nyogen Senzaki's loud and distracting party. All of this is just fine for finding your treasure, for realizing your true nature.

The reader is directed to Phillip McNamara's fine account in the appendix of how working with the koan "Who is hearing that sound" provided him with equilibrium in a period when he could have lost his sanity and literally his hearing.

Contemporary Sounds and Their Hazards

I must confess that, although I teach that we should be equally open to all sounds and unconditional in asking "Who hears?" in response to them, I struggle with the noise pollution of loud advertising on commercial radio and have been known to abandon my shopping basket full of groceries in the supermarket in the face of it. This is partly because such advertising is savagely compressed so that it comes out at twice the volume of the occasional music used to interrupt it. Along with the compression, all the pauses for breath are cut out of the ad to give it phony urgency. To hear it is to feel breathless and panicky, and against all reason I find it unbearable, even terrifying. When I mentioned this to Glenn Wallis, who teaches Zen in Dunedin, New Zealand, he responded: "Why not pause and take a couple of deep breaths on behalf of the loud voices that have no breath at all?"

So the loud and distracting party is a challenge; one reinforced by the likely presence of ubiquitous *doof doof* music with its computerized beat: an utterly regularized meter that is as far from the natural rhythms of the body as it is possible to imagine. Accordingly, I have a visceral fear of *doof doof* and its "regulated-by-the-studio-click-track" descendants.

My koan regarding such music and commercial radio advertising is, or at least should be:

Why not this too?

The Power of Music to Awaken Us

The music at the noisy distracting party is so loud it can break down our separation, for we are given no choice—short of noise-canceling headphones— whether we listen or not. It is good to ask, "Who hears?" nonetheless. Who is the one being deafened by the *doof doof* thump? And who is the one who hears those drunks boasting about their new yachts?

What is your treasure in the din of that party?

Dust on a Ruined Piano 23

While in Kyoto, I took a copy of *Zen Dust* to Daitokuji, hoping to leave it for the First Zen Institute there. However, the place was all rather sad looking and closed up, so I gave the copy to the abbot of Daisen-in, Ozeki Soen. His first words were: "What is this you've got—a Bible?" A most charming encounter with a crazy abbot . . . what dust . . . what mirror . . . how can dust ever settle on a ruined piano?
—OLIVIER BURCKHARDT

An Introduction to Ruined Piano

MY LIFE as a musician has been informed and shaped by Zen practice. In fact, much of the music I have created would have been unthinkable without it. In saying this, I speak for the power and virtue of zazen, whose effects are incalculable. Beyond that, metaphors of the Way have often been an inspiration for the musical structures and procedures that I have employed in my compositions, most specifically those involving ruined piano, the medium in which I have created the bulk of my work.

Metaphors for Emptiness

In my book *Dongshan's Five Ranks*, I wrote that "ruined piano" belongs with those other dead-end metaphors for emptiness, such as the stringless lute and the iron flute with no holes. A piano abandoned in nature becomes intimate with its environment. As its soundboard opens wider to show the cloudless sky, and a dusty wisteria clambers over its broken hammers, then the undefended piano that is no longer a piano is so open at the edges that everything and everyone can come through, can come in. And they do—yapping sheepdogs, trucks revving up, sheep-station owners complaining about the drought, roosters crowing in some out-of-joint time, all singing the 108,000 tongues of the Buddha through the empty dilapidated windows of one long ringing plucked bass string. To experience this, listen to my piece "Unfinished Business" on YouTube.

Ruth Fuller Sasaki and Zen Dust

Ruth Fuller Sasaki (1892–1967) was a pivotal figure in the emergence of Zen Buddhism in the West, and her pioneering translations have been an inestimable gift to Western teachers and students of the Zen Way. These include *The Record of Lin-chi*, *The Recorded Sayings of Layman P'ang* and *Zen Dust: The History of the Koan and Koan Study in Rinzai (Lin-chi) Zen*. Coauthored with Isshu Miura, *Zen Dust* was originally published in Kyoto in 1966 by the First Zen Institute of America in Japan, and by Harcourt, Brace & World in New York in 1967. *Zen Dust* is still the major resource in the West for understanding the history and nature of the koan as it comes down to us from China and Japan.

My early encounters with *Zen Dust* were through precious photocopies given to me by my teachers, Robert Aitken and John Tarrant, and it was my favorite reading in the early days of my Zen practice and study. Later it was a source and inspiration for my teaching, as well as for my book on the Five Ranks of Dongshan.

I am drawn to *Zen Dust*'s lengthy notes with their myriad stories and summations of key Chan and Zen texts, and I continue to find exploring this vast mine to be a source of wonder. Over the years I have made photocopies of my photocopied versions of *Zen Dust* for my successors as a transmission gift, as well as sharing copies with enthusiastic students.

I was delighted when Peter Wong Yih-Jiun, my co-translator on *Dongshan's Five Ranks*, told me that Olivier Burckhardt's Quirin Press was going to publish an updated edition of *Zen Dust*. I hastened to buy copies of the new edition from Olivier. Meanwhile, Peter sent him a copy of my double album of ruined piano pieces, *Frontier Piano* (2014). Olivier enjoyed the album and responded with the story that is the source for this chapter's koan: "How can dust settle on a ruined piano?"

That the abbot pretends to confuse Olivier's gift of *Zen Dust* with a Bible is a fine cross-cultural joke; one heightened by the fact that Olivier was returning *Zen Dust* to its source, because the First Zen Institute of America in Japan, at Daitokuji, was where Ruth Fuller Sasaki worked on *Zen Dust* in the first place. All this humor is heightened by the fact that *Zen Dust* is a compendium of wisdom regarding the koan and its role in the history of the Rinzai Sect, which is Ozeki Soen's own tradition. So much for him conflating *Zen Dust* with a Bible!

How Can Dust Settle on a Ruined Piano?

In Isshu Miura and Ruth Fuller Sasaki's *Zen Dust* we learn that "dust" is an old Chan metaphor for phenomena: the stuff of the world as we experience it through our senses. The six dusts are sight, sound, smell, taste, touch, and thought, and their domain is the phenomenal world. The Chinese interpreted the term "dust" to mean "that which defiles the pure mind," where "pure mind" evokes the sense of boundless empty mind.

Olivier's reference to the mirror and to the dust draws on an old Zen story I will briefly recount. To do this I will draw in turn on Robert Aitken's splendid telling of this story in his *Gateless Barrier*.

Huineng (638–713), who became the Sixth Ancestor, was a poor, uneducated layperson living at Xinzhou in the south of China. He gathered firewood and sold it to support his widowed mother. He had an awakening on hearing a monk chanting a line from the Diamond Sutra: "Dwell nowhere and bring forth that mind." Huineng approached the monk and asked him who his teacher might be. The monk replied that his teacher, the Fifth Ancestor Daman Hongren (601–674) lived a thousand or more miles away in the north of China. Huineng made the long journey to meet Hongren at Huangmei Monastery. After their dialogue, which convinced the old teacher of the young layman's ability, Hongren assigned Huineng to work in the rice-threshing shed.

At this time Hongren wanted to appoint a successor and set up a competition, saying: "Whoever believes he is worthy of transmission should submit a poem showing his insight into the essential matter, and I will acknowledge the author of the most cogent poem as the next master in our line." Yuquan Shenxiu (606?–706) was regarded by the community as the most realized of the monks, so the challenge of writing the poem fell to him. However, he wasn't sure of his own attainment, and after going thirteen times to Hongren's room to present his poem, he finally wrote it anonymously on a wall. His poem read:

> The body is the bodhi tree;
> the mind is like a clear mirror;
> moment by moment, wipe the mirror
>   carefully;
> let there be no dust upon it.

Hongren approved of the poem and had all his monks commit it to memory. However, he said nothing about making its author his successor. Huineng saw the poem and asked a monk to read it to him. Realizing the limitations of its author's realization, he dictated his own poem, which the monk also wrote on the wall. Huineng's poem read:

> Bodhi really has no tree;
> the mirror too has no stand;

from the beginning there's nothing at all;
where can any dust alight?

When Hongren read the poem, he said that it was of no value and erased it with his slipper. However, that night he visited Huineng in the rice-threshing shed and confirmed his realization. Then, he gave him the Precepts as well as the robe and bowl symbolizing Huineng's Transmission as the Sixth Ancestor. Because of the jealousy of the monks, Hongren advised Huineng to flee the monastery: "If you stay here, your life hangs by a thread." He even offered to row Huineng across the lake to ensure that he got away. There's much more to this splendid story, but the foregoing gives the gist.

The meaning of "dust" in both poems is not so much "the senses of sight, hearing, smelling, tasting, and touching," as it is the sixth sense of "thoughts and thinking." "Wiping the mirror" is clearing the mind mirror of thoughts, and the practice of counting the breath, for example, is a means to this. On the other hand, Huineng, in his poem, presents the absolute where there is nothing at all from the beginning. So how in that timeless, dimensionless realm can there be thinking or conception, trees or mirrors, for each and all of these are without abiding self? It is Huineng's cracked, indeed ruined, theme that Olivier Burckhardt's question takes up:

How can dust ever settle on a ruined piano?

INVESTIGATION 12: *Vertical and Horizontal Time*

The notion of "vertical time" has become popular in spiritual circles in recent times. Vertical time is experienced in moments that seem absolute: a snail clinging to the piano's back, the sight of my grandchild approaching, a drink of water. These moments cannot be further divided. Within vertical time there is no past or future. The haiku moment is surely in vertical time. It is late spring here in Western Australia, jacaranda time:

> all at once
> the jacarandas' mauve
> hazes the slopes

"Horizontal time" on the other hand involves a past that is remembered and a future that is imagined, expected, and perhaps hoped for. Horizontal time is linear, unfolding in measured sequence from past to present to future, or—if you prefer—the reverse: from future to present to past. Horizontal time corresponds to our mundane, conventional notion of time; it is the time by which we live, or the cage in which we live and die.

If we extend the imagery of "horizontal" and "vertical" to Zen, each or any moment of horizontal time is, potentially, the timeless moment of vertical time: the same timeless moment that doesn't come marked as past, present, or future, that doesn't come and go at all.

In the above account from yogic traditions, the vertical moment is privileged, but in Zen we deal with the moment without fear or favor, which is to say that we don't cling to special states and conditions, we don't cultivate epiphanies; we just respond as the moment requires. When it is time to feed our cat, we feed our cat; when the time comes for our vehicle to be serviced, we make the appointment. Like this, any moment, no matter how mundane, conveys—indeed *is* not other than—the timeless vastness. The grandeur of life, the miracle of our lives is not elsewhere.

A *tick* of the clock swallows all notions of vertical and horizontal time. Who are you at such a moment?

Phillip McNamara's "How to Catch a Fish" 24

When I was young, my uncle would take me fishing along small creeks. The streams would mostly dry up in summer except for a couple of pools. I had many questions about the wonder of these pools. I was told that they were unimaginably deep and that though divers had gone down to find out why the pools never dried up, the bottom had never been reached. I could see they were not wide enough for a submarine to explore. But I imagined that even a submarine would never reach the bottom. My uncle said that the best fish lay in holes deep in those pools that never dried up. I was too scared to ever swim in them like he did, but I liked to imagine that one day I'd get a fishing line long enough to catch that fish.

—PHILLIP MCNAMARA

PHILLIP MCNAMARA is a devoted student of the Zen Way and a long-term Zen practitioner and leader in the Zen Group of Western Australia. The mythic story he shares above is expressive of the Way in its limitless depth and inexhaustibility, while the presence of his uncle who can swim in those holes that never dry up and who passes on the wisdom regarding where to find the best fish exemplifies the way you plumb the depths of a koan with your teacher as guide.

We can admire the humor of the fishing line that Phillip wishes for: one so long that its reach exceeds the depths that can be reached by divers, or even by submarines.

It is right that Phillip's uncle passes on the wisdom to his nephew in the form of a tall story. The use of fantasy to engage a child's imagination is perfect—perennial in fact—for it never ceases to engage us as adults. The true grown-up never grows up. Who hasn't been hooked by those lines from the opening chapter of Lewis Carroll's 1865 *Alice's Adventures in Wonderland*?

> The rabbit-hole went straight on like a tunnel for some way, and then dipped suddenly down, so suddenly that Alice had not a moment to think about stopping herself before she found herself falling down what seemed to be a very deep well. Either the well was very deep, or she fell very slowly, for she had plenty of time as she went down to look about her, and to wonder what was going to happen next.

How can we not want to know what happens next?

The passing on of stories is important for us all. Often, we do it through family and thereby weave the past into the present and pass on stories to our sons and daughters, and our grandchildren, who in the future will, in their turn, pass those stories on to their offspring.

In times that seem increasingly ahistorical, there is an avid interest in family history, perhaps in reaction to a kind of vapid "nowness" that is encouraged by social media and the Internet generally. In this regard, there is a popular program on Australian television that traces the ancestry of celebrities. We actually get to watch how moved or disturbed they are when they discover what their ancestors got up to: all those jail sentences, illicit relationships, illegitimate children, and tragic deaths. The program is called—perhaps aptly in terms of the themes of this book—*Who Do You Think You Are?*

The Zen Way comes down to us partly through stories, and this is especially true of the koan path itself. In its best expression, Zen is rarely literal—I am tempted to say, never literal. The opening of the *Song of Enlightenment*, a poem usually attributed to Yongjia Xuanjue (665–713), reads:

> There is the leisurely one,
> Walking the Tao, beyond philosophy,
> Not avoiding fantasy, not seeking truth.

In Zen we don't seek literal truth; rather, we seek the mythic as it comes to us through images and archetypes—whatever will inspire our lives and encourage us to deepen in the Way and to awaken. Phillip's account, with its elements of mystery and fantasy, is just such an archetypal story.

How do you catch the fish that inhabits the fathomless depths?

INVESTIGATION 13: *Timeless Life*

With the maturing of the Way comes the realization that time is a concept we use in order to be able to describe change in a changing world. However, the deeper we live the Way, the more the concept of time—including its passage and measurement—vanishes off the margins of our experience, and the moment, in its vastness, emerges as our true face and being. Yet, perforce, we live by measured time; we live by the clock.

In social and professional terms, we have little or no choice about this.

How, in a life dominated by the clock, can you manifest your true and timeless nature?

> Most of our difficulties, our hopes, and our worries are empty fantasies. Nothing has ever existed except this moment. That's all there is. That's all we are. Yet most human beings spend 50 to 90 percent or more of their time in their imagination, living in fantasy. We think about what has happened to us, what might have happened, how we feel about it, how we should be different, how others should be different, how it's all a shame, and on and on; it's all fantasy, all imagination. Memory is imagination. Every memory that we stick to devastates our life.
>
> —CHARLOTTE JOKO BECK

CHARLOTTE JOKO BECK had such a scorched-earth approach to memory. For her, memory is merely imagination, which is to say that we make up the past: airbrushing it, amplifying the good bits while trying to suppress the painful parts, all the while being haunted by its traumas. Regarding this, the French have an expression: *l'esprit de l'escalier*—"the spirit of the staircase"—which manifests, for instance, after you have been insulted in the apartment above, and you think of the perfect riposte on the staircase on your way out. Alas, its moment has passed, and you can't return to triumphantly deliver it.

As Joko puts it: "Nothing has ever existed except this

moment." Memory unfolds now—in this moment—
just as anticipation and planning unfold now.

How Avoidance Shapes Our Lives

The ghostly imaginary past can overwhelm the present.
This occurs, for instance, when our memory of being
taunted or insulted causes us to avoid the offender in
the present. Thich Nhat Hanh invites us to see the ways
our avoidance shapes our lives. Looking down, we see
our patterns of avoidance as a maze of scuff marks
crisscrossing in the dirt—tracks obscuring tracks—as
we fearfully shape our present circumstances to avoid
some humiliating encounter we had long ago. This is
how memory sticks to us and molds our lives. On the
other hand, we tend to cling to memories of past happiness and seek comfort and consolation in those memories. Acknowledging this, Dante wrote that the most
poignant sorrow of all is to recall happiness in times
of misery. Understandably, much literature is rooted in
the loamy soil of memory, inadvertently giving support
to Joko's tart observation: "Memory is imagination."

Indeed, it is true that we create an imaginary self
and its story out of our memories. And we cling to
that ghostly self, just as we cling to the memories that
help to reify it.

Still, a memory can be a Dharma gate: an opening
to the Way—not less than a ray of sunlight falling on
a pewter mug.

How can memory be a Dharma gate?

INVESTIGATION 14: *Intimacy across Time*

The present is an inconceivable, unlivable point between a past that is gone and a future that is not yet. Yet we live this moment as timeless. This moment—what is it for you right now?—doesn't come marked as "past," "present," or "future." Such labels may be vitally necessary for us to orient ourselves in time, but in terms of the deepest reality they are subsumed by this moment in its vastness. Yet we can give sense to the passage of time, and we do. Time's passage—which evokes contingency, karma, and timefulness—and the timelessness of the moment that is no other than the universe, which is not other than you yourself, correspond to each other. In the spirit of the Middle Way, you can't have one without the other. If you evoke time, timelessness tags along—not a breath between them.

Throughout this book we are concerned with the theme of *intimacy across time*, most especially in those circumstances when a moment or even an extended period of experience from the apparent past is not other than the present moment. Such an experience may grant us freedom from the order of linear time. This is not an experience of the past as it is *remembered* in the present; it is an embodied experience of the past *in* the present, of *the past as the present.*

Experiences of *intimacy across time*, as with

synchronicities, are like sparks from the conflagration of our timeless essential nature.

How does your timeless essential nature manifest right now?

We are all time beings: each of us is the gathering of past, present, and future. At the same time, we are all for the time being. When we are no longer, the wind that lifts the ocean waves will still be, as will the stars. And over the longest time, they will depart.

The passage of time is inexorable. We know this on our pulses. We are all marked with our own decline, and our mortality presses hard. That all things pass quickly away—that we pass quickly away—is the Buddhist family story endlessly told and retold, because in some sense we don't want to get it.

It is tempting to see the passing of time with our attendant experiences of old age, sickness, and death as the only story in town; however, there is an "and yet" to this story. We find an account of this in the essay *Uji* (*The Time-Being*) by the Japanese Zen master Eihei Dogen (1200–1253). For Dogen we are all for the time being—which is to say, fleeting and transient—yet in the same breath we are, each and all, intimate with the timeless moment in its vastness. In fact we are not other than it.

Since there is nothing but just this moment, the time-being is all the time there is. Grass-being, form-being are both time.

Each moment is all being, is the entire world. Reflect now whether any being or any world is left out of the present moment.

Each of us is just this moment; each of us is all the time there is. There is no time left out of the present moment, including time past and time future. Because of this there is no come and go of time. In the following passage, Dogen makes this explicit:

> Yet yesterday and today are both in the moment when you directly enter the mountains and see thousands and myriads of peaks. Yesterday's time and today's time do not go away. As time is not marked by coming and going, the moment you climbed the mountain is the time-being right now.

Time passes; yet, in the same breath, time does not come and go, which is to say, the moment in its timeless vastness does not come and go. This latter is the "and yet" to the impermanence story, its hidden face. The time of past experience is not other than the time being right now. We are not other than this moment; we are timeless, even as we travel inexorably towards death.

An Experience of Intimacy across Time

Kathy Shiels—a devoted student of the Zen Way and a long-term practitioner and leader in the Zen Group of Western Australia—wrote to me about her experience of how "the moment you climbed the mountain is the time being right now." Kathy recounts her experience of intimacy across time—of the past as present—seamlessly and beautifully, as follows:

In terms of conventional time, it was a little after ten o'clock, at South Beach, on a Tuesday morning in January. There were only a few people walking or swimming under the cloudless sky. My dog and I had rippled enough laps through the mirror of the Indian Ocean, so, avoiding patches of dried seaweed, we traipsed past the sea heath up the gentle dune. There was no one else at the beach shower, so we took our time. Following the toweling-dry ritual, we wandered to a grassy area around the sole peppermint tree. Ella, my old dog, dropped to the grass like a bag of bones and gazed out at the ocean.

I stood in the sunshine following her gaze and was about to lay out a towel in the dappled shade of the peppermint when my toes became younger by decades. Tuesday morning dissolved into childhood ground. The boundless blues of sea and sky and long white stretch of almost empty beach became the shore of sandcastles. With wet hair plastered down my back I crouched on that shore and plunged my freckled hands into a soggy hole that was quickly filling with water. Clasping the sodden sand between water-shrivelled fingers, I bent lower and carefully dripped the next turret onto my castle as the sun beat on my shoulders and back. Higher, higher, higher the turret rose until stealthily the sea slid towards it and claimed its base. Down it tumbled. I gasped, but my sun-burnt legs welcomed the cool swoosh of the easing wave. The sea breeze arrived with its salty taste playing tunes of muffled calls, tinkling rigging, and seagull screeches. My hands, washed of all days and age, lunged at the wet sand again ready to forge another castle base.

Ella woofed her demand for her usual post-swim treats and I turned towards her as my arthritic fingers fossicked in the beach bag.

Kathy's experience speaks so clearly and movingly for itself that I am reluctant to comment. All that I would venture to say is that when past and present are intimate to each other, as in Kathy's experience, this has nothing to do with memory. The time of her past experience is simply not other than her time of right now.

What is your experience of intimacy across time?

WE ALL GET to experience in measure: conditional love, unconditional love, true love, false love, love as lust, lust as love, tough love, tender love—not forgetting cupboard love—and I wonder, given the diverse forms of love, if there can be any encapsulating koan with love as its theme.

We mostly think of love in human-to-human terms, but what about the love of animals? Also what about those forms of love that go out beyond the love of individual creatures and animate service to others, service to the planet? What of the love that fosters and is fostered by artistic creation?

Whatever the profusion of love's forms, there is no getting away from its primacy. Gary Wallace, a student of the Zen Way, offers the following koan concerning our relationships with others:

We spend so much time trying to get away from others, so as to avoid the pain of relationship. Only to find that the other that one has been trying to get away from is none other than our self. And then to realize that the only way to get away from self is to be with others.

We touched on the essential notion that "the other is not other than ourselves" in our earlier account of the koan "When you're making love, who is the other?" As we saw, the experience of love and sex can be a path to realizing our true nature and an intimate expression of it. Like this, sexual intimacy and intimacy with reality as a whole are intertwined. Yet the experience of being thus in relationship also embraces our differences; at the outset we may spend our days and nights together, but in time each of us may have our own plan for how we will spend the day and our plans may be grounds for disagreement. Just our disagreement also includes—and is not other than—what is timeless and without limit.

Moreover, when we are alone and burdened by our separateness, our aloneness is still a vehicle for the Way, since those others—blue sky, red hibiscus, the autumn sun radiantly reflected in the puddle—convey us perfectly.

When I was young, I was in love with romantic love in all its unconditional splendor. With age, I've come to see love as mortal and mostly conditional. For all the purity of heart and sacrifice, there is always a trace of taking advantage of the other and being taken advantage of. With love deepened by age and experience, this is accepted both ways. Sexual love, or plain lust, is mostly the easy part. To endure the difficulties of a protracted relationship without giving up on it; to accept the other as who they are, and to endure the loneliness and bitterness that often lie at the heart of aging marriages and relationships form one of the hardest challenges that we may face.

What Is Love?

With the breakup of a long relationship, the things I most missed were those I used to do for the other person. These were things that at the time when we were together may have felt merely dutiful: picking them up from work, for example. This is not to say that I didn't miss the things that were done for me, but the feeling of love—its lightness and uplift, its simplicity—lay chiefly with what I was able to offer in the time of the relationship.

This is not to say that getting our needs met is unimportant, and it's hard to imagine a viable relationship where this can't happen at least somewhat. But the truths of love lie deeper than merely getting what we want.

In some measure when we attend to the other person we lose our self-preoccupation, and with that—over time and without our wishing and willing it—there comes a measure of release and lightness, a joy that cannot be gainsaid. This has nothing to do with feeling or being virtuous or good. Even in the depths of what is broken, there resides love that, light and gracious, feels free from the vicissitudes of time and circumstance.

We have no trouble recognizing our own unique visage in the glowering mirror, yet who is it that we see? And—when we dutifully set down tools to pick up our "better half" from work—who is the other?

IF AWAKENING is the honeymoon of the Way, enlightenment is the marriage. When we speak of awakening, we are referring to our first opening to the Way: the first glimpse of our self-nature. When we speak of enlightenment, we are referring to the maturing of our awakening: our gradual embodiment of it, our learning to express it, and finally, when it is absorbed into our least activity, our forgetting it so utterly that we live it—or, more properly, it lives us. At that point, enlightenment is nothing other than our ordinary activity: sleeping, waking up in the morning, getting out of bed, going to the toilet, doing zazen, and drinking a first cup of coffee for the day—as it always has been. It is also doing what must be done. When my two-year-old granddaughter ran off, leaving me unable to stop her getting on the railway station escalator rising towards her, all I could do was to shout "Rose!" as she teetered on the edge of those lethal metal steps. "Rose!!" And that stopped her.

"Enlightenment is as enlightenment does" is inspired by the old expression "Handsome is as handsome does," where your attractiveness rests not so much on your looks, as on how well you treat others.

Our enlightenment, correspondingly, resides in our activity and how it impacts the world.

How do you live "Enlightenment is as enlightenment does"?

INVESTIGATION 15: *Punctuality*

Zen is precise about time, so much so that in the beginning years of practice, I thought that only those with good time management would get to experience eternity. When Robert Aitken came to Western Australia, I took him sightseeing. We were running late to pick up the senior student from Sydney who was helping organize our first sesshin with a teacher. As we took in the view of the city, I asked Robert Aitken, "How do I show my family this splendor?"

"Be punctual," he replied.

What is the splendor?

> Mole spoke up after a long silence one
> evening and asked, "What's compassion?"
> Raven said, "That's an inside story."
> Mole asked, "Inside what?"
> Raven said, "Stars on your fur."
> —*ZEN MASTER RAVEN*

IN HIS BOOK *Zen Master Raven*, Robert Aitken (1917–2010) presents his insights gleaned from a lifetime of study, practice, and the teaching of the Zen Way "through the beaks and muzzles of the creatures of the forest," as Nelson Foster so aptly puts it in his foreword. By so doing, Robert Aitken—or Aitken Roshi, as we affectionately knew him—created his own discourse record, but one with a difference. Rather than literally setting forth his exchanges with students—the quintessential responses he had made, or wished he had made, to their questions, over decades of teaching—he playfully recasts those exchanges as dialogues between the creatures of the forest and their teacher, Zen Master Raven. This was his quirky, ingenious, and modest way of presenting his own discourse record.

Foster suggests that we read Robert Aitken's *Zen Master Raven* "simultaneously as a serious record of his six decades practicing and eventually teaching Zen and as a lark, a merry improvisation by an old man living in retirement, entertaining himself and fully intending to entertain others as he set forth the path of liberation."

Although the dialogues in *Zen Master Raven* have a familiar and homey feel, Aitken Roshi's presentation of the Dharma in the exchanges between Zen Master Raven, that wise old bird, and the other creatures in his assembly is subtle—"corner of the mouth" in style—and gives nothing away.

Aitken Roshi wrote that koans are the folk stories of Zen, and on at least one occasion he referred to *Zen Master Raven* as a book of koans. Taking him at his word, I have chosen one of the dialogues—in this instance, between Zen Master Raven and Mole—to see what it might yield as a koan.

What Is Compassion?

Mole is one of the students in Zen Master Raven's Sangha. He's thoughtful, compassionate, respectful, and very concerned about the suffering of others. Several of his questions arise from a long silence—befitting a mole—as in the present instance when he asks Raven: "What's compassion?"

Mole may have hoped that Raven would give him an explanation of compassion along the lines of "suffering with others with a strong urge to help them." Even to say "compassion" softens the heart-mind and body. But saying "compassion" doesn't make us compassionate, any more than feeling the warm glow of a compassionate impulse need result in compassionate action.

In the not-quite-post-Romantic West we place a high value on feeling and sincerity, which is to say, if you are going to act compassionately, you've got to mean it, you've got to feel it. But compassion is mostly doing what needs to be done: helping your neighbor to start their car or kneeling to tie a child's shoelace with or without the accompanying warm glow.

Compassion, however conceived, releases us from our self-preoccupation and is hopefully helpful to those we attend. Mole may have been seeking such an account of compassion from Raven to inspire him into helping the creatures of the forest to better their lives.

Who benefits from your compassion?

An Inside Story

Raven's reply to Mole's question regarding the nature of compassion comes as a shock, for it has its source in a deeper place: the origin of compassion and compassionate activity itself.

An inside story is one known only to those close in; an inside story is an intimate matter: in fact, as Raven is expressing it, the innermost matter. When we experience who we truly are, that experience is utterly intimate and personal, yet in the same breath it is completely open to all: the wind moves the branches of the cape lilac, the pink hibiscus blossoms shake as the wrens and New Holland honeyeaters get busy at nectar. With "That's an inside story" Raven conveys the vastness of who we truly are and presents it in the same breath.

Mole responds: "Inside what?"

Such an innocent question, such a great question. Unknowingly, Mole presents the innermost matter. Imagine sitting out under the night sky with is spattered stars and a cool breeze blowing. In just that place, I ask you: "What is the inside of *this*?"

Raven replied: "Stars on your fur."

He deeply acknowledges Mole's, "Inside what?" and presents the immensity of our true and timeless nature right there. What does this have to do with compassion? Raven's very words are an intimate act of compassion; they are intimacy in all its dark radiance. Truly the stars are closer than our breathing, and the night moves on little feet—or big feet, depending.

Mari Rhydwen's "Thank You"

Words themselves may constitute the vastness of our true and timeless nature, in which instance they are no longer solely words. Even a single word can be thus, as Mari Rhydwen's interjection in the following story, shows:

> Mari Rhydwen, Glenn Wallis, Arthur Wells, and I were giving an evening of short talks for students in Glenn Wallis's dojo in Dunedin after teaching sesshin there. I gave one on gratitude, which was warmed by the fact that I had mislaid my wallet

several times that day—and found it again. Each time I had it back in my hand I'd mumble, "Thank you, Universe." I continued, "I'm sure there must be a better way to express that." Mari chimed in, "Thank you."

"Thank you" enfolds the universe. On another occasion, Glenn Wallis conveyed this same matter when he said: "My words are not what I am saying."

Coda

Mole came to Raven privately and said, "We haven't talked about death very much. I'm not concerned about where I will go, but watching so many family members die, I'm wondering what happens at the point of death?"

Raven sat silently for a while, then said, "I give away my belongings."

Back in 2010 I was engaged in an email dialogue with Aitken Roshi. Our exchange concerned the concluding lines of Dongshan's poem, "The Song of the Precious Mirror Samadhi":

> Conceal your practice, function in secret,
> seem for all the world like a fool or an idiot—
> if you could only continue, it would be called
> the host within the host.

I had sent him a copy of Peter Wong's and my translation of the poem. Roshi said that he liked our translation and sent back his own, which he said he also liked. However, the last line about the host within the host was missing in his translation. I asked him—it was irresistible—"So what is the host within the host, Roshi?" "I'll get back to you on that," he emailed back.

Shortly after, I heard that he had died.

His "I'll get back to you on that" was a perfect reply—Raven incarnate—even without his obliterating follow-up.

Where is Roshi now?

INVESTIGATION 16: *Everyone Is Doing Their Best*

Nothing lasts, including us. We're all just for the time being. This isn't solely a personal consideration, it's also a shared one. Nothing lasts, and we're all in it together, as Robert Aitken wrote.

The fact that our lives are finite suggests that we should make the most of the time we have, even though we mostly don't know how much that is: finding time to love and to express our love; finding time to finish business, to seek forgiveness and to forgive; to create while there is time.

And if we fail to do any of this? Joko Beck wrote: "Everyone is doing their best." Even the most wretched life, a life that seems to abjectly fail—cut short by drug abuse or dealing—still embodies the vastness, graces the planet.

Everyone is doing their best.

Who Dies? 30

SURELY, this is a no-brainer and can't be considered a koan at all. I will die; you will die. We all will die, regardless of our opinions about death, and no matter how hard we work to prevent it. Death comes to all of us, regardless of our wish to endure just a little longer: to savor the love we give and receive or to complete the book of our life. In the face of death, all these are as nothing. Yet we live for the most part in denial of the certain certainty of our death, even though across the world 51,600 people die each day—that being 55.3 million people who die worldwide in a year. Even though we know intellectually that we will inevitably die, it is hard to stare into that sun.

The Fear of Death

Stephen Levine in his excellent book *Who Dies?* asks:

> Who is prepared to die? Who has lived so fully that they are not threatened by their imaginings of nonexistence? For it is only *the idea of death* that frightens us. It is the unknown we pull back from.

However, even with deep realization, we may still fear death: not so much the fear of the immense unknown that is death and dying, but the impact of our death on our families and the difficult legacy that our death may leave them. Correspondingly, we may fear the death of those we love more than our own death. My greatest fear is that my children, or grandchildren, will predecease me.

We may fear dying more than death itself, with its pain, loss of control, and the indignity that goes with that. This is also true of the long goodbye of Alzheimer's disease, which is a death before the fact and rightly to be dreaded. These fears are certainly both real and rational. Moreover, we mostly have no say over how we die or the timing of our death, and our first night nerves can start years in advance.

All I Can Do

All I can do is be me, whoever that is.
　　　　—BOB DYLAN, IN AN INTERVIEW

We all die—and yet there is a part of us that believes that our existence is, in the same breath, timeless, edgeless, and that we are the good friend of forever. It all depends on what we understand as "who." If we take the low road, "who" is any one of us in our ordinary attachment to our names and roles, avidly cultivating "the me that isn't there"—and feeling entirely vulnerable, as well we might. If we take the high road, then we are not limited by our skin or our skull; we are not even limited by our ideas about who we think we are. In the spirit of the high-road, in your 5'6" (name your own height!) body the universe comes and goes. We can get a taste of this through the experience of Pedro Rojo, a Zen student of Daniel Terragno's and mine, from Chile. Pedro lived in Western Australia with his family for five years and was an inspiration for the practice of the Way in our Sangha. He told me the following story:

> After dropping my son at school, I turned on the ignition in my car—the radio was already on, and it was Vivaldi. I knew the melody and I knew how it continues, naturally without effort it felt a part of me—and all of a sudden I was living in the music, the music was me. I felt that my intimacy with the music made me the music, so much so that even if I died, a part of me would still remain in the music and that music would be myself. I don't care if I die. Even if I die I am living as that music. I thought it was interesting to think that I won't ever die because I am more than myself. Although of course no doubt I will die.
>
> I write to you to remember it [this experience] and because I thought that there is something there, something of our practice . . .

Who dies?

HERE'S THE OPENING of a poem of mine:

ANNIVERSARY

Missed visiting your grave Dad, too busy
too caught in ambition so that studio follies
ate the fortune that you stowed—twenty
    thousand in lobsters
caught between the pages of *The Cruel Sea*
    or *Bhowani Junction*
or floating down with dust from the pockets
    of your trousers
hung upside down inside your darkened lowboy.
I spend you thin then thinner, finally return to
    where
we laid you low, stand in the muggy afternoon
to ask my daughter "Where's he gone?"
to hear her say "Good question, Dad."
Where have you gone? . . .

MY DAUGHTER AMANDA worked for many years with
Amnesty International and was their national secre-
tary for part of that time. She worked hard to alleviate
the suffering of refugees here in Western Australia and
others feeling the weight of injustice worldwide. She

is an inspiration to me and shows me how to live the Zen Way.

After my father died, I was slow to visit his grave. Finally, Amanda and I got there, and after the long pause that indicates respect, but also bafflement, I asked Amanda: "Where's he gone?" Amanda replied, "Good question, Dad."

Religions tell a story about what happens after we die: we may be reborn—we hope favorably—or be reunited with God. These stories give comfort to believers and are an important reason why religions continue to hold sway in the world. On the other hand, from a secular materialist perspective, death ends all; whoever or whatever we take ourselves to be perishes along with our body, and in this we go the way of all other sentient beings. Finally, however—regardless of our religious convictions or philosophical positions— we really don't know what happens after we die.

The Japanese Zen master Hakuin Ekaku (1686– 1769) embellishes this theme a little more than is commonly suspected:

> A student asked Hakuin, "Where do we go after we die?"
>
> He responded, "I don't know."
>
> The student retorted, "But you're a great Zen master."
>
> "But not a dead one," Hakuin replied.

Hakuin's "I don't know," means what it says, yet in the same breath, his "I don't know" gathers the timeless immensity that is life and death and even what may follow death.

My old accordion teacher, Harry Bluck, who gave so much support and encouragement to young musicians including myself and fought for the rights of West Australian musicians through the Musicians' Union, said in an oral history interview recording that he made shortly after he turned seventy:

> As far as a religious hereafter is concerned I've had a strong idea in my own mind that our hereafter is what you make it while you're here. I mightn't be explaining that too well. A lot of the influence that one wields—doesn't matter how close it is, whether it's just family, or the like—the hereafter part is what you do while you're here, and that's where I feel the best part of the contribution comes in.

In terms of what we do while we're here, Harry surely had in mind compassionate action on behalf of others, and that for him is the hereafter itself in its best form. Whatever is hereafter is what we do here, what we express and enact now.

Amanda's "Good question, Dad" gathers up the humid gray autumn day, the grave, and us all. This may not alleviate grief and sorrow, but grief and sorrow are also gathered in as "Good question, Dad."

Where do you go after you die?

INVESTIGATION 17: *One Moment Is Enough for All Time*

Although our character develops incrementally, sometimes our fate is decided in an instant. Falling in love can be like this, artistic inspiration and religious conversion, likewise.

I remember as an eleven-year-old watching some older boys playing Australian Rules Football at the local park. One boy took a high mark, which is to say that he leapt high in the air over his opponents' heads to capture the ball. He was wearing the red and white colors of the South Fremantle Football Club, a team that was nicknamed "the blood-stained angels." That moment overturned my heart, and I instantly became a Souths supporter, which is to say that I was converted to a club remote from where I lived and that had many immigrant players from countries like the former Yugoslavia, which made my choice incomprehensible to my parents. Over the ensuing years I would travel religiously each Saturday to watch my heroes John Gerovich and Tom Grljusich play. Even these days, in winter, I buy Monday's *West Australian* newspaper to check "how South went."

Our character develops from the myriad small decisions we make in our lives on a daily, even hourly basis, yet there are decisive moments that illuminate who we are and what we may become. The small decisions that develop character are usually forgotten; the single instant of illumination, rarely. Such moments feel timeless because they gather a past and future of their own into themselves, drawing together the fragmentary impressions and straggling associations of life and giving them significance, as well as karmic potency.

Isn't any moment up for this?

Carpe Diem and the Pursuit of Happiness 32

TRULY, all things pass quickly away. Our lives are fleeting, and all too soon we will die. The Roman poet Horace (65–8 BCE) summed up the necessity for us to make the most of time and maximize our opportunities for pleasure—especially the pleasures of love and sex, of living well—with his terse injunction: *Carpe diem* (Seize the day).

Yet, how difficult it is to seize the day. We can't even seize the moment, for suddenly—ludicrously—there is the moment and someone trying to grab hold of it. *How can you grab hold of what you already are?*

We can't lay hold of the future, either. The future is not yet, and in an important sense it will only ever come into its own as the present. We may have hopes for the future, but whatever hopes we have for it unfold now. We can't preempt it either. I remember a man who wanted to show our family his moonflowers. The vines still hadn't flowered, so he ripped open the shoots to show us the partly formed blossoms. As we left, my children kept saying, "Ridiculous, ridiculous." It was difficult not to agree with them.

The Pursuit of Happiness

The notion of *the pursuit of happiness* arises readily from "seize the day." However, happiness pursued tends to be particularly elusive. I'm reminded of the powerful and moving ending to F. Scott Fitzgerald's *The Great Gatsby*:

> And as I sat there brooding on the old, unknown world, I thought of Gatsby's wonder when he first picked out the green light at the end of Daisy's dock. He had come a long way to this blue lawn, and his dream must have seemed so close that he could hardly fail to grasp it. He did not know that it was already behind him, somewhere back in that vast obscurity beyond the city, where the dark fields of the republic rolled on under the night. Gatsby believed in the green light, the orgastic future that year by year recedes before us. It eluded us then, but that's no matter—tomorrow we will run faster, stretch our arms further . . . And one fine morning—So we beat on, boats against the current, borne back ceaselessly into the past.

Our hopeless striving to capture the future while being borne back ceaselessly into the past is an image for our times, so geared to acquisition, to getting and spending, even while at unprecedented speed we and all that we grasp for are consigned to oblivion.

Of course, we need to care for our life, and it is understandable that we want to get our needs met and be happy in love, as well as being comfortably well off. At the same time, there is a way to settle deeper in to our lives: a way that allows us to be with others and with our environment without that grasping for love, money, or the power and control implicit in "seize the day" or "the pursuit of happiness."

> Leaving aside the pursuit of happiness, how do you live it?

INVESTIGATION 18: *Hume's Piece of Coal*

When we are ideologically driven and prone to rant, it is good to remember that the harder we try to drive our position home, the more inclined its opposite is likely to appear, if not in our own heart, then in the silence of our friends.

There is a story about the Enlightenment philosopher David Hume (1711–1776) that exemplifies this. Hume was most likely an atheist, but he came to dislike the rant of the Atheist's Club that he frequented as a young man when he lived in Paris, so he stopped attending. Years later when Hume was dying his friends gathered around him. James Boswell, Samuel Johnson's biographer, asked Hume: "David, what chance of an afterlife?" Hume replied: "The same chance that that piece of coal won't ignite if you place it on the fire."

If you had been there, how would you have responded to Hume, beyond empirically testing his response?

JORGE LUIS BORGES (1899–1986) was born in Buenos
Aires and educated in Europe. From 1955 to 1973 he
was the director of the Argentinian National Library.
Borges wrote primarily short narratives, poems, and
brief essays, yet, as André Maurois put it: "Because of
their wonderful intelligence, their wealth of invention
and their taut, almost mathematical style they suffice
for us to call him great."

In his essay, delightfully and paradoxically named
"A New Refutation of Time," from his book *Labyrinths*, Borges summons up a scenario where the precise repetition of any moment in the linear sequence of
time is sufficient to dissolve that sequence and demon-
strate that both the sequence and the continuity of time
are unreal. Borges employs what we are encouraged
to accept as a vivid personal experience of eternity to
illustrate his point about the unreality of the sequence
of time. An examination of this experience will enable
us to further investigate the theme of *intimacy across
time* we have been exploring throughout this book.

The location for Borges's experience is a suburb of
Buenos Aires not far from where the author (or his
fictional self) had grown up:

The street was one of low houses and though its first meaning was one of poverty, its second was certainly one of contentment. It was as humble and enchanting as anything could be. None of the houses dared open itself to the street; the fig tree darkened over the corner; the little arched door-ways—higher than the taut outlines of the walls—seemed wrought from the same infinite substance of the night. The sidewalk formed an escarpment over the street; the street was of elemental earth, the earth of an as yet unconquered America. Farther down the alleyway, already open to the pampa, crumbled into the Maldonado. Above the turbid and chaotic earth, a rose-coloured wall seemed not to house the moonlight, but rather to effuse an intimate light of its own. There can be no way of naming tenderness than that soft rose colour.

I kept looking at this simplicity. I thought, surely out loud: "This is the same as thirty years ago . . ." I conjectured the date: a recent time in other countries, but now quite remote in this changeable part of the world. Perhaps a bird was singing and for it I felt a tiny affection, the same size as the bird; but the most certain thing was that in this now vertiginous silence there was no other sound than the intemporal one of the crick-ets. The easy thought "I am in the eighteen nine-ties" ceased to be a few approximate words and was deepened into a reality. I felt dead, I felt as an abstract spectator of the world; an indefinite fear imbued with science, which is the best clarity of metaphysics. I did not think that I had returned upstream on the supposed waters of Time; rather I suspected that I was the possessor of a reticent or absent sense of the inconceivable word "eternity."

"The infinite substance of the night," "this now vertiginous silence," the sound of the crickets drained of time, and the protagonist who feels "dead" are all intimations of emptiness. The phrase "a reticent or absent sense of the inconceivable word 'eternity'" speaks for a timelessness beyond words and concepts. The notion of eternity in play here is not that of infinite temporal duration, but of timelessness. Borges continues:

> I write it now as follows: That pure presentation of homogenous objects—the night in serenity, a limpid little wall, the provincial scent of honeysuckle, the elemental earth—is not merely identical to the one present on that corner so many years ago; it is, without resemblances or repetitions, the very same. Time, if we can intuitively grasp such an identity, is a delusion: *the difference and inseparability* of one moment belonging to its apparent past from another belonging to its apparent present is sufficient to disintegrate it.

It is not that the moment of past time and the moment of present time are connected through memory, as associations; rather, each moment is *identical* to the other. Is this one, or is this two?

Within that timeless moment—"that pure presentation of homogenous objects—the night in serenity, a limpid little wall, the provincial scent of honeysuckle, the elemental earth"—the past is not other than the present; the present is precisely the past. In this, they are like a single mirror reflecting itself. (Borges's "that pure presentation of homogenous objects" eloquently evokes the timeless emptiness of the "night in serenity" and all that it holds.) At the same time, Borges's play with "past moment" and "present moment" in terms of "difference" and "inseparability" is revealing. If I understand him correctly, it is not only the *inseparability* of past and present moments that dissolves linear time, it is also, paradoxically, the *difference* between those moments that does likewise. Understood this way, each unique moment is completely timeless and unconfined: the moment of humid breathlessness no less than the moment of spring breeze.

Inseparability and *difference*—like emptiness and form, absolute and relative, essential and contingent—are the polarities of the Zen Way, which is beyond polarities; they include each other and at the same time are no other than each other. This is ensured by the vastness of this moment that readily embraces past, present, and future, and where duration and sequence have no purchase. Does that mean we still have our breakfast before our lunch? When there is breakfast, there is only breakfast. Nothing is vaster than breakfast.

We live by the clock, or more likely these days, the screen on our mobile phone. (He who lives by the phone, dies by the phone!) On being asked "What is the time?" an Australian child of fifty years ago might have said, looking down at their wrist, "A hair past a freckle." "A hair past a freckle" neatly encompasses past, present, and future. Even the less vivid, and perhaps more helpful, "Three thirty" cuts off all considerations of before and after.

Borges writes that time is a delusion. How do you square that with the realities of your daily schedule and the appointments that you make and keep?

INVESTIGATION 19: *Involuntary Memory*

The country of the past may return to us through what Proust called "involuntary memory," which is to say that aspect of memory that occurs when cues—especially sensory ones like smell and taste, but also hearing and seeing—evoke a recollection of the past without any conscious effort on our part. We all experience involuntary memory: a musty smell brings back the classroom that we knew as a five-year-old; the smell of smoke and the way that smoke deepens the sun's glow bring with it the feeling of living on the edge of the bush as a child; or a pop anthem evokes the pains and joys of our youth or even the image of our first love.

We all know this, but for the most part we tend to make no claims concerning the nature of time based on such experiences. That being said, apart from the grandeur of the literary experience that Proust affords us, his employment of "involuntary memory" and the transcendent experiences that may be triggered by it amount to the Dharma, which enlivens us, extends us, and pushes back the boundaries imposed on us by our own ignorance.

What is your experience of involuntary memory? Does it evoke a sense of the timeless in your life?

Proust's "Freed from the Order of Time" 34

> One minute freed from the order of time has recreated in us,
> in order to feel it, the person freed from the order of time.
> —MARCEL PROUST

GENUINE REALIZATION is not limited by the time barrier, or indeed by barriers of culture. Our true self, normally buried under daily fears, concerns, and preoccupations, is set free when the sequence and order of linear time is transcended, and we experience the past as intimate with the present. In order to explore this notion of *intimacy across time*, I have chosen as a koan for this chapter a quotation from late in Proust's great novel *À la recherche du temps perdu* (*Remembrance of Things Past*). Published in its complete form in 1927, five years after Proust's death, *Remembrance of Things Past* is a towering masterpiece and surely *the* oceanic novel of the twentieth century, perhaps of all time, in its range and depth. Despite its length, the rewards of reading it are immense, for its psychological depth and insight into the human heart put it on a par with Shakespeare and Tolstoy.

In *Remembrance of Things Past* Proust evokes the decline of a titled and entitled aristocracy in France during *la belle époque* (roughly 1870 to 1914), with a deadly eye but understanding heart. *Remembrance of Things Past* explores the ravages of aging, illness, and death and is a remorseless study of the fading of beauty, the loss of illusions about love, and the vanity of our hopes and wishes. As such, it is consonant with the traditional Buddhist themes of impermanence and suffering.

However, impermanence is only one part of the story—albeit the major one—because within the labyrinthine plot of *Remembrance of Things Past* are occasions when the linear sequence gives way to *moments bienheureux* (fortunate moments). These "fortunate moments" convey a liberation from passing time and its destructive power; they represent *an experience of intimacy across time*: an intimacy that collapses time, such that the past supplants the present or hovers within the present—or the past is the present. (Proust employs these diverse clusterings of past and present variously in the assorted "fortunate moments.") With his experience of such moments, Proust's protagonist Marcel is, momentarily at least, freed from the order of time. With them his true and genuine self—unconfined by chronometric time—is set free.

The Taste of a Madeleine Dipped in Lime Tea

Any moment may be "fortunate," even the mundane moment of tasting a little cake (*une petite madeleine*) dipped in lime tea, which—without Marcel wishing or willing it—grants him an experience of timelessness as it resurrects his childhood. Marcel's experiences of the timeless typically arrive when he is least expecting them, when he is feeling about as far from transcendence as it is possible to feel:

> And soon, mechanically, weary after a dull day with the prospect of a depressing morrow, I raised to my lips a spoonful of the tea in which I had soaked a morsel of the cake. No sooner had the warm liquid, and the crumbs with it, touched my palate than a shudder ran through my whole body, and I stopped, intent on the extraordinary changes that were taking place. An exquisite pleasure had invaded my senses, but individual, detached, with no suggestion of its origin. And at once the vicissitudes of life had become indifferent to me, its disasters innocuous, its brevity illusory. This new sensation having had on me the effect which love had of filling me with a precious essence; or rather this essence was not in me, it was myself. I had ceased now to feel mediocre, accidental, mortal. Where could it have come to me, this all-powerful joy? I was conscious that it was connected with the taste of tea and cake, but that it infinitely transcended those savours, could not, indeed, be of the same nature as theirs. Whence did it come? What did it signify? How could I seize upon it and define it?

We're never privy to the source of this precious essence. But it overturns everything. The intellect tries to close on it, but it's beyond meaning and definition. Once we are touched by it, we are shaken up and transformed in our depths. And indeed, as Proust has his protagonist express it: "this essence was not in me, it was myself." This is our true self—customarily buried under daily fears, concerns, and self-preoccupation—which is set free when past and present are intimate to each other.

The Past within the Present: Freedom from the Order of Time

Marcel's experience on tasting the madeleine occurs early on in the novel. Thousands of pages later, in the midst of a cluster of "fortunate moments," we encounter the following extraordinary passage, from which I have extracted the koan that we are investigating:

> One minute freed from the order of time has recreated in us, in order to feel it, the man freed from the order of time. And because of that we can understand why he trusts his joy, and even if the simple taste of a madeleine does not seem logically to contain reasons for this joy, we can understand how the word "death" has no meaning for him: situated outside time, why should he fear for the future?

With such an experience of intimacy across time—one minute in duration for Proust and briefer for most students of the Way—there is recreated in us, in order that we might genuinely experience it, the person freed from the order of time.

Implicit in Proust's account of "the person freed from the order of time" is the suggestion that our true nature consists of being free from time's tyranny and that as we age and are corrupted by the world, we lose contact with the timeless essence that is in fact us. When we encounter our timeless essence, the word "death" has no meaning for us, and if we are "situated outside time"—which is to say that we are not other than the moment in its vastness—why indeed would we fear for the future? We are already it.

Our experience of bodily change and its irreversibility persuades us that time is passing. We see this in ourselves, and we see it in others. All of us are immersed in the mundane stream of birth and death, where we are swept up to death's wall to be frisked and finally robbed of all that we have. In these senses the passage of time, which has all things passing away, is unquestionable, even axiomatic.

We are all subject to the ravages of passing time, and yet it is precisely in the midst of change and decline that we experience liberation from it. Any moment in time's passage is—immediately—"the moment of all moments" whether we are there for it, or not—and we are mostly not.

Unfolding the Dharma of the Taste of a Madeleine Dipped in Lime Tea

Proust's account of Marcel's experience on tasting the madeleine dipped in lime tea accords with how we discover the Way as our life. After his initial experience on tasting the few morsels of cake soaked in lime tea, Marcel investigates the experience, attempting to renew it. However, each time he tastes the tea it gives diminishing returns. He ponders:

> It is plain that the object of my quest, the truth, lies not in the cup but in myself . . . I put down my cup and examine my own mind. It is for it to discover the truth. But how?

Surely, the truth lies within himself, not in the cup. The path opens right there with that insight.

Examination of one's mind is a good first step, but the truth is not within the reach of the intellect, as Proust demonstrates when he embarks on a remorseless analysis of the limitations of the intellect as it strives to come to terms with this profound experience. He tries to see how some moment from the dead past might have connected with the ecstasy occasioned by tasting a crumb of the madeleine, and this has him on the edge of abandoning his quest.

> Ten times over I must essay the task, must lean over the abyss. And each time the natural laziness which deters us from every difficult enterprise, every work of importance, has urged me to leave the thing alone, to drink my tea and to think merely of the worries of today and of my hopes for tomorrow, which let themselves be pondered over without effort or distress of mind.

Read for us ordinary students of the Way, "Thousands of times I must essay the task, must lean over the abyss." As for Proust, or rather his protagonist, our natural laziness ensures our sliding away from the enterprise. Where do we slip away to? However, as true students of the Way, we return over and over again, and this goes on beyond any reason.

Then suddenly the memory returns. It was of that little crumb of madeleine which on Sunday mornings at Combray when I went to say good day to her in her bedroom, my Aunt Leonie used to give me, dipping it first in her own cup of real or lime-flower tea. With that recognition . . . immediately the old gray house upon the street, where her room was, rose up like the scenery of a theatre to attach itself to the little pavilion opening on to the garden, which had been built out behind it for my parents (the isolated panel which until that moment had been all that I could see); and with the house the town, from morning till night and in all weathers, the Square where I was sent before luncheon, the streets along which I used to run errands, the country roads we took to when it was fine. And just as the Japanese amuse themselves by filling a porcelain bowl with water and steeping in it little crumbs of paper which until then are without character or form, but, the moment they become wet, stretch themselves and bend, take on colour and distinctive shape, become flowers or houses or people, permanent and recognizable, so in that moment all the flowers in our garden and in M. Swann's park, and the water-lilies on the Vivonne and the good folk of the village and their little dwellings and the parish church and the whole of Combray and of its surroundings, taking their proper shapes and growing solid, sprang into being, town and gardens alike, from my cup of tea.

The vivid reality of Combray resurrected is timeless. The past comes to life as the present, even as it transcends both past and present. In terms of Proust's novelistic vision, it provides a foreglimpse of the quest and the immense journey to reclaim the past that is *À la recherche du temps perdu*. However, Proust, consummate artist that he is, doesn't dwell on this experience; rather he immediately plunges his protagonist back into the dissatisfactions and unrequitements of his mundane life. Likewise we let go of our own glimpses of the timeless and enter again the riptides of our daily life. We can't and shouldn't contrive to sustain the harmony.

"One minute freed from the order of time has recreated in us, in order to feel it, the person freed from the order of time"—how do you manifest your own freedom from the order of time?

The Future in the Present 35

THAT THE PRESENT moment has an ambit claim on the span of our life—indeed of all life—is well summed up by Joko Beck's "Nothing has ever existed except this moment. That's all there is. That's all we are." Throughout our investigations of the timeless yet fleeting moment, we have given sense to the notion of the past within the present; now let us look at the less likely notion of the future in the present. To do so, I will draw on a story from J. B. Priestley's book *Man and Time*, one that tells of the experience of a pilot in World War II—unnamed in Priestley's account—that gives vivid life to the notion of the future in the present:

In his childhood and youth during the 1930s in England he suffered attacks lasting a day or so, keeping him prostrate with blinding headaches and nausea. Lying in a darkened room, toward the end of each attack he would experience a kind of passage "through a succession of colors, so vivid that they hurt—the reds, blues, greens, and purples merged and wavered," then they would separate and seem to submerge him in the intensity of their glare. At this point, he would feel fully awake and would vomit, and then sleep long and soundly and awake feeling refreshed and quite well.

Years later, in World War II, he was with the R.A.F. in Malaya. Japanese fighter planes attacked a convoy he was traveling with in the mountains. He and the other men were ordered to scatter in the surrounding jungle. He recounts what happened, as follows:

> As I burst through the green maze I saw a small ravine below me, occupied by Australian machine-gunners. A Jap fighter, swooping low, seemed to be following me with personal intent, and I dived into the security of a ravine. In that moment the world exploded into a hell of color. All the jagged splinters of red, blue, green, and vivid purples caught and swamped me and flung me among the gunners.

A bomb in fact had burst just behind him and blown him into the ravine. The next thing he knew he was being violently sick. Later he was taken prisoner. But never again did he have the old attacks, or see the bright menacing colors, and then be sick.

Priestley himself comments that the early events in this man's story became an elaborate foreshadowing of what happened in Malaya; they were almost like rehearsals for it. Or we can say that the effect of those few minutes in the jungle was so powerful that just as it haunts him now, long after the event, so too it haunted him long before the event.

We have seen how an epiphany may carry its own past and present within itself, as in the red and white "blood-stained angel" story earlier. While the protagonist's devastating experience is an unlikely candidate for an epiphany, it does embrace a past and a future; it does involve *intimacy across time.*

When we are intimate with the moment, we are intimate with the totality, which includes past and future, just as that explosion—the world as a hell of red, blue, green, purple—gathers foresense and memory into itself and, fundamentally, is not other than our own true nature.

How can you prove this?

INVESTIGATION 20: *Who Is Judging?*

The Zen Way is comprehensive, and it surely includes our imperfections, and indeed our demons. We deepen in the Way when we begin to accept our imperfections and face up to our demons. When we can own these, we can more readily accept those of others. As it is, we tend to judge ourselves harshly—something that can readily be confirmed by listening in on our vicious self-talk when we screw up.

Correspondingly, we judge ourselves equally so.

Judgment of others (if not of ourselves) involves creating the scenario of self and other. If you want to subvert that dualism and heal that separation, ask yourself: "Who is judging?" This is a fine koan for the thick of our lives.

Who is judging?

Time that is moved by little fidget wheels
Is not my time, the flood that does not flow.
Between the double and the single bell
Of a ship's hour, between a round of bells
From the dark warship riding there below,
I have lived many lives, and this one life
Of Joe, long dead, who lives between five bells.
—KENNETH SLESSOR

KENNETH SLESSOR (1901–1971) is one of Australia's finest poets. His celebrated poem "Five Bells" is arguably the greatest Australian poem. In the opening lines of "Five Bells" above Slessor eschews linear clock time (the "time that is moved by little fidget wheels") in favor of time envisaged as "the flood that does not flow," which is to say a notion of time beyond any sense of movement or passage.

Time as evoked by Slessor conveys such dammed-up immensity and is a compelling image for the encompassing moment where—between the bell strikes of a ship's hour—the poet lives many lives, as well as the one life of that roistering wild boy, Joe Lynch. On May 14, 1927, Joe fell overboard from a ferry en route to a party and drowned in Sydney Harbor.

Slessor's great poem, written nearly a decade after

his friend Joe's death, is saturated with the feeling and sense of the Way, especially in its opening and conclusion. In his notes on "Five Bells" Slessor writes:

> Many hundreds of years ago in an Arabian fairytale, a man dipped his head into a basin of magic water. In the few moments between submerging his face and withdrawing it, he dreamed that he had sailed on seven voyages, and was cast up in a shipwreck, captured by pirates, discovered a diamond as big as a turkey's egg, married a princess, fought in many battles, and was brought to execution.
>
> After he had lived this whole lifetime, he opened his eyes and shook the water from his face and found himself amongst a laughing group of people, with everything around him exactly as it had been before he had dipped his head in the water five seconds before.

Slessor uses this story to exemplify the theme of "a lifetime in a moment"—a prominent matter in this book—to evoke the notion that the whole span of a human life can be imagined and even vicariously experienced in a flash of thought as brief as the three-second interval between the double *ding-ding* and the single *ding* of the ship's bell. Within that interval, a sequence from a very different time scale is interposed, compressing about thirty years of human life into those three seconds.

The words "five bells" are repeated three times in the poem to indicate the three decades of Joe's life and, as Slessor puts it: "to remind the reader that time, on the other scale, has occupied only a few moments, that the tongue of the bell is still moving and the sound is still suspended in the air." This "double exposure" aptly evokes the image of the moment that includes our lifetime and the lifetimes of countless others, which we have been investigating in the course of this book. It is important to note that Slessor retains the actuality of linear chronometric time throughout by stressing the presence of the bells from the darkened warship. Thus, although he inclines to time as the flood that does not flow—time in its absolute mode—he maintains the presence of time in its mundane aspect as well. It is important that both perspectives are present, as the mutual interdependence of the timeless and the timeful conveys the depth and richness of awakened experience, and how we live it.

> I looked out my window in the dark
> At waves with diamond quills and combs
>   of light
> That arched their mackerel-backs and smacked
>   the sand
> In the moon's drench, that straight enormous
>   glaze,
> And ships far off asleep, and Harbour-buoys
> Tossing their fireballs wearily each to each,
> And tried to hear your voice, but all I heard

Was a boat's whistle, and the scraping squeal
Of seabirds' voices far away, and bells,
Five bells. Five bells coldly ringing out.

Five bells.

These concluding lines of the poem are so affecting.
Joe is unreachable in death. The poet cannot hear Joe's
voice, for the gap between the living and the dead cannot be bridged, yet the sound of the boat's whistle, the
seabird's voices, and the five bells coldly ringing out are
in the deepest sense drawing us into timeless intimacy.

In this we are all true contemporaries.

How is this so?

INVESTIGATION 21: *Time and Music*

If we regard the present moment solely as that infinitesimal point where the past becomes the future or the future turns into the past, there can be no music. For music to be, we need a more expansive moment. Correspondingly, music creates the moment on a more lavish scale, such that when we hear two notes in succession we anticipate the third or, more likely, the rest of the phrase and beyond. Like this, the music breathes its way into an imaginary "not yet," even as it is creating it. And it does this while retaining its past at least in vestigial form. Mozart wrote to his father that he would walk out after dinner and conceive a symphony in its entirety, with "all its parts sounding at once." His only task then, was, on his return home, to laboriously write it all out!

Music unfolds in time, creating the illusion of its flow. It can slow time or speed it up, and this doesn't necessarily depend on the music being slow or fast, either. Music can create the motionless moment, the still core of things, even as it is that. Music bends time. Works such as the Beethoven late piano sonatas and string quartets and, say, Olivier Messiaen's *Quatuor pour la fin du temps* (*Quartet for the End of Time*) are meditations that transform us if we are prepared to give them our undivided attention, our deep listening.

The ubiquity of music, especially through the Internet, has done music a huge disservice. I remember an acquaintance of mine saying that it was good to work from home because he could have "wall-to-wall music." I can't think of anything worse. I seek out restaurants that don't have music. The Viet Hoa restaurant in Perth, Western Australia, is my idea of paradise. There is no music; peoples' conversation, the waitresses talking in Vietnamese, and the sounds and smells from the kitchen mingle so happily that, if after I die, I have the chance to return, this is a place where I would feel at home.

Music takes time, like love takes time. These days it seems that nobody has time to listen, really, as they listlessly flick from track to track on Spotify or YouTube. Or the music is allowed to play on without anyone attending to it, such that timeless works are turned into high-quality noise pollution.

Why not spend an hour listening intently, undividedly, to music you love.

Who are you at such a time?

> My great day came and went, I do not know how.
> Because it did not pass through dawn when it
> came, nor through dusk when it went.
> —ANTONIO PORCHIA

ANTONIO PORCHIA WAS born in Italy in 1885, but after the death of his father in 1900, he emigrated with his mother and six siblings to Argentina. To earn a living and support his family, Porchia worked for many years as a basket weaver and stevedore in the Buenos Aires port. In 1918 he and his brother bought a printing press in the city, where Porchia would be employed for the rest of his working life.

Porchia wrote a book in Spanish entitled *Voces (Voices)*, a book of aphorisms, so called—Porchia is reported to have said, "Never say I write aphorisms, I would be humiliated." Ever since they were self-published in 1943, Porchia's writings have defied classification. What are these brief texts? And how could there be no name for something so utterly recognizable?

"Night Is a World Lit by Itself"

Roberto Juarroz, the renowned Argentine poet and one of Porchia's closest friends, once wrote that the "voices," as Porchia called them, were perhaps simply "depth": that was all, "depth itself." "*Voices* is almost a biography," Porchia once said, "which almost belongs to everyone." Porchia's odd brief texts were not written *for* or *toward* something, but simply *as* something.

> Even the smallest of creatures carries the sun
> in its eyes.

> A hundred years die in a moment, just as
> a moment dies in a moment.

In this spirit, Porchia's "voices" shine with Zen.

My great day came and went, I do not know how. Because it did not pass through dawn when it came, nor through dusk when it went.

"My great day" conveys the sense of a special or memorable day, a day long awaited—a day longed for. Such days pass, and pass all too quickly. Porchia refers to his great day, but in Zen terms "the great day" is each or any day, even a day when we feel miserable, confined, and cold. On such a day, the glory is not elsewhere—the rain darkens the veranda, my feet are cold. There is the haunting sense that Porchia with his image of the great day is invoking our life, which does not pass through childhood nor through old age.

The passing of Porchia's great day evokes the world of contingency: his great day's uniqueness, its singular unrepeatability. At the same time, the day's not passing through dawn and not passing through dusk evokes the timeless.

The day does not pass through dawn: dawn is the matter entire; the day does not pass through dusk: dusk is the matter entire. Yet somehow the day passed, though Porchia does not know how. His *not knowing how* is the dusk sky with Venus rising; it is dawn with Venus the last star shining as the sun rises.

How can this day—great, or otherwise—be said to pass?

Fionn's "The Finest Music in the World" 38

There is an old Irish story of the hero Fionn mac Cumhaill. Fionn asks his followers, "What is the finest music in the world?" They suggest answers: the cuckoo calling from the hedge, the ring of a spear on a shield, the song of the lark, the baying of a pack of hounds, the laughter of a gleeful girl or the whisper of a beloved. "All good music," agrees Fionn. "But what is best?" they ask. Fionn answers: "The music of what happens is the finest music in the world."

UNLIKE THE MOVIES, life has no pre-composed music. Your heart gets broken, but the strings don't swell empathetically.

The finest music in the world goes on beyond the ordinary canons of musical beauty and profundity: tonight it's the song of the earth—the night hum of cities, industrial sounds, shouts, cries of pain, pleasure, laughter; the sounds of being born mingling with the sounds of dying; the hum and roar of traffic, *doof-doof*, a Mendelssohn quartet playing around the pumps in the late-night service station; digital beeps in the library, people chatting happily over a meal in the Vietnamese restaurant, the smack of surf on the beach, a jet opening up the sky; and, closer in, the thump of the plumbing in the old house, trees being moved about in the night wind, night birds' song; and, closer in still, your beating heart. The finest music in the world offers itself unstintingly.

Yet this is *not* Fionn's meaning, which points us beyond any literal account of sound and music. The music of what happens may include the sounds and music of the world and yet is . . .

What is the finest music in the world?

JOE HARDING is a long-term student of the Zen Way and a stalwart of the Zen Group of Western Australia. He is a true person of the Way. Joe had gone to Queensland to pick up an old bus for his tour service in Margaret River, some 170 miles south of Perth, the West Australian capital. On the way back—approximately halfway through the immense journey of some 2,500 miles—his bus broke down in Port Pirie, South Australia, and this is where Joe's story picks up:

Sitting early morning zazen by the mangroves of Port Pirie, the smoke of bushfires in the hills across the inlet drifting up towards the blue desert sky, already hot in a series of very hot days. My circumstances stranger than fiction and bleakly mirrored as I fill in days waiting for an alternator for my old bus that has the guys in the workshop scratching their heads and making calls to all kinds of places, including Japan where there's rumoured to be one out there still, somewhere in the country.

I hear from out of the mangroves a man singing in a voice raspy with years of champion ruby smokes, but with flamboyant gusto "oh what a beautiful mornin', oh what a beautiful day, I've

got a beautiful feeling everything's going my way."
He does its ebullience justice, but doesn't follow it
up with the other lines—he just leaves it hanging
in the air, until a crow picks it up and flies off.

I hurriedly finish my zazen and turn to look
for the source of this mysterious voice and expect
to see the man, perhaps sitting behind me on a
bench, but there is no one there. He is as invisible
as the crickets that are already in high volume on
this hot morning, and my cries of "hello, hello"
draw the same response of emptiness, silence,
before the chirping begins again. It is going to be
another very hot day so I get up and return to the
motel room to wait for any news from the garage,
and watch the updates on the bushfires that are
burning tenaciously all around us.

The next morning I again make my way to the
mangroves to sit zazen, the heat has subsided and
a fine drizzle of gray warm rain descends in gentle
curtains across the smoldering landscape. It is the
blessing that the people of Port Pirie have been
praying for and I can almost hear the sizzle as
fires in the distant hills begin to sputter and die.

I settle into sitting and towards the end of my
round the man begins to sing those famous lines
again "oh what a beautiful mornin', oh what a
beautiful day, I've got a beautiful feeling everything's going my way." As with yesterday he is
nowhere to be seen, the gray green mangroves
keep him hidden and mysterious: he is there, but
not there to be seen. I imagine him sitting there

in his mangrove dojo, the warm rain beading in his tobacco-stained beard, a twinkle in his eyes.

I know better than to call out again, seeking an answer, and instead make my way back through the drizzle to the motel room to wait for any news from the garage, and flick through the coverage of the fires, though this time the desperation to get going the way I always intended to has strangely left me.

Commentary on Joe Harding's Story

In the middle of the waiting, in the middle of the heat and the threat of bushfires, Joe hears the song carried by the tobacco-roughened voice coming out of the mangroves—"oh what a beautiful mornin', oh what a beautiful day, I've got a beautiful feeling everything's going my way"—which of course it isn't!

Port Pirie under threat of bushfires is a long way from the brimming optimism of the opening song from Rodgers and Hammerstein's musical, *Oklahoma*. Moreover, the sentiment of the song is remote from Joe's difficult, even dangerous circumstances and his pressing need to get going, to get home. As Joe expresses it: "The song is present as a fragment, the man is invisible as the crickets that are already in high volume on the hot morning." Joe's cries of "hello, hello" draw the same response of emptiness, silence . . . All this evokes the depths, the mysterious source of who we truly are.

On the second morning it rains, and Joe beautifully describes the blessing of that rain bringing with it the abatement of the threat of the bushfires ringing the town.

And in his zazen is the song arising: "Oh what a beautiful mornin' . . ."

Who is hearing that? Who is that?

This time Joe does not respond with an answering call of "hello, hello." There is surely no need to.

The ending of Joe's story is very soft: his desperation to get going has strangely left him. What is it that holds him?

The song is hidden: the heart of the Way is in hiding. Yet it is as clear and bright as a crow's *caaark*, as the rain beading in the man's tobacco-stained beard. The song is ancient, and it sings regardless of our hopes and fears; it sings even as our hopes and fears.

What is the heart of the Way in Joe's story?

William Blake's "Eternity Is in Love with the Productions of Time" 40

To see the world in a grain of sand,
And a heaven in a wild flower,
Hold infinity in the palm of your hand,
And eternity in an hour.
—WILLIAM BLAKE

THE POETRY AND prose of William Blake (1757–1827) provide us with a rich array of koans. These lines from his "Auguries of Innocence" are well known and each line can be investigated as a koan. The last, in particular, evokes the spirit of this chapter's memorably beautiful koan "Eternity is in love with the productions of time": one of Blake's "Proverbs of Hell" from his book *The Marriage of Heaven and Hell*. Blake's words convey the intimacy of the timeless and the timeful, which has been one of the central themes of this book.

From Blake's perspective eternity is heaven: remote and inaccessible, while the productions of time—representing all that is mortal and changeable—are hell. Hell, as conceived by Blake, is a radical departure from the conventional Christian hell as a place of fire and damnation; for Blake it was the realm of creative energies: sensual, spontaneous, and all about desire and the human body.

For present purposes, I understand "eternity" to mean "timeless," rather than its familiar sense of "infinite duration." Thus we can express Blake's line as "the timeless is in love with the productions of time."

Blake wrote that "Without Contraries is no progression." And the "Proverbs of Hell" present us with various "contraries":

> The road of excess leads to the palace of
> wisdom.
> Excess of sorrow laughs. Excess of joy weeps.

Then there is the achieved union of contraries:

> The pride of the peacock is the glory of God.
> The lust of the goat is the bounty of God.
> The wrath of the lion is the wisdom of God.
> The nakedness of woman is the work of God.

Maturity in Zen involves us in being able to hold the tension of opposites, and indeed deepening in the Way makes this more than possible. Like this, the opposing pulls of desire and restraint we feel in the presence of someone we are strongly attracted to can ripen into open-hearted acceptance and love.

In the vastness of who we truly are, the polarities of our nature find their home: invoke time, and timelessness appears; invoke the eternal, and there is our life with its steady parade of weddings and funerals— not forgetting our early morning cups of coffee. In the deepest aspect, timelessness has no other means to express itself than through our life in time as it is shaped by Eros and sexual desire. In this regard, what is whole, pure, and eternal may be imagined to struggle to express itself through intimacy with all that which is mortal and fallible. And yet, finally there is no evidence of a struggle at all.

Eternity is in love with the productions of time. How do you respond?

Summing Up:
A Conspectus of the Time Themes

WE BEGAN our investigations into the nature of time with the fundamental question, "What is time?" along with its adjunct question, "What if there is no such thing as time?" We then proceeded to investigate the theme of *intimacy across time* through koans such as "Who are your true contemporaries?" and by investigating various insights into the nature of time—chiefly around the themes of *the past within the present* and *the past as the present*, as they occur in the writings of Dogen and the literary works of Borges, Slessor, and Proust.

A prevailing theme of this book has been the timeless immensity of this fleeting moment, which gathers in the limitless past and unimaginable future, while being not other than each of us: equally timeless, yet transient.

The contingent aspects of time—its passage, flow, duration, and measurement—have also had their place in this account, and this most especially in our investigation of Heraclitus's koan: "You never step into the same river twice, for fresh waters are always flowing in upon you," where we paid tribute to the passage of time and, accordingly, to the ever-shifting nature of the self. At the same time we noted that Heraclitus's fragment, "We step, and we do not step; we are, and we are not," pays tribute to the timeless empty realm, even as it acknowledges contingency and change: being and becoming without a breath between them.

Taking all of this together:

What is time?

Coda: A Fantasia on Popular Melodies—
Five Koans on the Theme of Music

1. *Rhapsody in Blue*

I LEARNED the piano accordion from the gifted young
virtuoso Giuseppe de Sondrio. He'd sit at his big black
desk, looking out over rusting rooftops to the Town
Hall clock, which would finally chime out the end of
my lesson. Meanwhile he labored at his arrangement
of George Gershwin's *Rhapsody in Blue* for accordion
and orchestra, filling up the close-printed orchestral
score with his bold elegant notation. As I stubbornly
learned to play Schubert's *Serenade*, *Rhapsody in Blue*
piled towards completion on the left side of his desk.
No matter how badly I played the serenade, I could
never disturb his perfect concentration.

2. *Last Long Look*

There's hardly anything that I can recall of the six
years ("the formative years") I spent playing piano at
the Parmelia Hilton's Garden Restaurant. Maybe only
that night when a businessman, after rummaging for
something in the inside breast pocket of his suit coat,
tumbled backwards off his chair onto the deep red
thick pile carpet. Ray, the bandleader, said, "Just keep
playing." The waiters rushed in a shoji to screen off the
body. The drunken head wine waiter gave him mouth-

to-mouth resuscitation. Patrons no more than three feet away, affecting not to notice, burrowed deeper into their lobster mornays. Even today I wonder what was the last tune the businessman heard in this life. Was it "More" or was it "Cabaret"?

3. *The Left Hand of God*

At the Federal Hotel, I heard John Gill, West Australia's legendary ragtime pianist, play rags by Scott Joplin, as well as early jazz by Jelly Roll Morton. During John's break, I climbed up on the barstool beside him and asked him, admiringly, "How did you get to play like that?" He blew the head of his pint of dark brown Dogbolter, waited a bit, then said: "You need the left hand of God."

4. *Tango*

On the rainy July morning of my eleventh birthday I was playing my accordion in the darkened lounge room. The doorbell announced sobbing voices. From behind their screen door my parents oh-noed as my aunt and uncle told their story, not quite drowned out by the rain's roaring. I kept playing the tango to show I wasn't listening, and to silence what I could hear too well. My tango protected the entire family. It tried not to hear of the death of my cousin.

5. Left-Hand Story

I was driving to Apparitions Fantasy Costume Shop to pick up a tuxedo large enough to contain my "paralyzed" right arm slung close to my heart, all for the midnight performance of my *Left Hand of the Universe* (simultaneous left-handed improvisations between musicians in Slovakia, Colorado, and Fremantle, West Australia). On my way to Apparitions I heard Beethoven's only violin concerto and remembered that, in the first poorly rehearsed performance, likewise just before Christmas some 190 years ago, Franz Clement was the soloist. It is said that he interpolated an improvisation on a one-stringed violin played upside down between the first two movements of Beethoven's concerto. John Boyden, the critic and historian, comments: "Just what he hoped to achieve from this circus stunt is difficult to imagine."

PART III

The Crow Flies Backwards
and Other Western Koans

Koans with a commentary in part 2 are marked with an asterisk.

*1. Who am I?

*2. "Save Me, Bill."
Tony Coote recounts this story. "An old school friend of mine was walking the Kokoda Track with friends. (The Kokoda Track is in Papua New Guinea, where Australians and Japanese fought in World War II.) One night they camped at this place along the track and my friend woke up hearing someone crying, "Save me, Bill."

The next morning they found spent rounds of ammunition on the ground at the campsite, and later still discovered that this was a place where Australians had been killed."

How do you save that ghost?

*3. Heraclitus's "Fresh Waters"
You never step into the same river twice,
for fresh waters are always flowing in upon you.

We step, and we do not step;
We are, and we are not.

*4. When you're making love, who is the other?

*5. Eduardo Galeano's "True Contemporaries"
However hurt and shattered one might be,
one can always find true contemporaries anywhere in time.

Who are your true contemporaries?

*6. Nyogen Senzaki's "Party"

When you are at a party that is very loud and distracting, just close your eyes for a moment, and you'll find your treasure is right there. At such a time, what is your treasure?

*7. Arthur Wells's "Blame"

Why does birth have to be so painful? I asked myself again and again, and the Darwinian answer is the only one that comes back—it is so painful because we stood up on two feet and grew very big heads that don't fit down through a narrow pelvis evolved for four-legged locomotion. Nobody planned this. Absolutely no one is to blame.

In Arthur's account, what is our true nature transcending Darwinism, theology, and their disputes?

*8. Rainer Maria Rilke's "Our Inner Seasons"

How we squander our hours of pain.
How we gaze beyond them into the bitter duration
to see if they have an end. Though they are really
seasons of us, our winter-enduring foliage, ponds,
meadows, our inborn landscape, where birds and
reed-dwelling creatures are at home.

What is your inborn landscape?

9. Aeschylus's "Acquisition of Wisdom" (adapted)

Even in our sleep, pain which cannot forget
falls drop by drop upon the heart, until
in our own despair, against our will, by the grace of
the Way comes wisdom.

*10. Why do we suffer?

*11. Anne Carson's "There is no person without a world."

*12. Nick Arnold's "What is the true value of your money?"

13. Who breathes?

14. Who is seeing?

15. Glenn Wallis's "What is the essential ground of all beings?"

*16. Issan Dorsey's "You get what you deserve, whether you deserve it or not."

*17. Grace

Grace under pressure: that ability to deal lightly and freely with what is difficult is a gauge of maturity on the Way. My father, while not a Zen practitioner in the formal sense, exemplified this most aptly for me. Always playful, he found the freedom and the grace to play, even in his pain and distress. When he was in his eighties, he was knocked down by a delivery van. In hospital they put him in "treatment," prior to admitting him as a patient. Although no one could find time to get him a bottle to piss in, four staff members came round with their clipboards during the three hours he waited there, to ask him his age. He generously gave each of them a fresh response—"twenty-one," "ninety-eight," "forty-seven," and finally, "two hundred!"

How can you find your own true and timeless nature in my father's joking responses to the ward staff?

THREE KOANS FROM AUSTRALIAN INDIGENOUS SOURCES

*18. The crow flies backwards.

19. Wakemab

Just off the eastern coast of Saibai Island, Torres Strait, northern Australia, the dinghy motor is cut. The fishermen nod in the shore's direction, acknowledging Wakemab, the beach that was once a man. "Is that Wakemab's place?" one asks of the other. The other replies, "Yes, he is a whirlpool, many miles distant."

20. The Master Song Man (John Tarrant's koan from Joan Sutherland's and John Tarrant's *A Zen Harvest*)

In Arnhem Land a man named Maralung was sleeping. In a dream, a master song man came to him and said, "Wake up, I have a song to teach you." At first there was a light approaching through the trees. But it became apparent that it was a human being. The dreamer woke up, and the master taught him the song. But then the dreamer went back to sleep and forgot the song. Next day the musicologist asked him for the song. So the next night Maralung dreamed again, and it happened the same way. Again the master came to him in his dream and taught him the song, while he was awake, and again he fell asleep afterwards. But in the morning he remembered the song.

So, was the master song man there or not?

THREE KOANS ON THE NATURE OF MIND

*21. Wandering in Your Mind
"Still wandering in your mind?" I asked a student.
"You bet."
"What's there?"
"Oh, gray sky, the sun on the salmon gums."

*22. Realizing the Nature of Mind
I asked a student, "Zen is the complete realization of mind—
what do you understand by that?"
    She responded, "I can have silly thoughts."

23. Rimbaud's "The Mind's Disorder"
Finally, I began to consider my mind's disorder sacred.
(*Je finis par trouver sacré le désordre de mon esprit.*)

••⤜ ⤛••

24. Descartes's *"Cogito, Ergo Sum"*
I think, therefore I am.

25. Arthur Rimbaud's *"Je est un autre"*
I is another.

*26. Joko Beck's "Don't be angry."

27. Amy Hollowell's "Who benefits from your generosity?"

28. Mary Oliver's "What is your place in the family of things?"

29. e e cummings's "Whatever we lose (like a you or a me) / it's always ourselves we find in the sea."

30. William Blake's "Grain of Sand"
To see the world in a grain of sand,
And a heaven in a wild flower,
Hold infinity in the palm of your hand,
And eternity in an hour.

31. Pablo Neruda's "When I awake who am I if I was not I while I slept?"

32. Christopher Brennan's "Clear Dusk"
I feel a peace fall in the heart
of the winds, and a clear dusk settle
somewhere far in me.

33. Wordsworth's "Impulse"
One impulse from a vernal wood
May teach you more of man,
Of moral evil and of good,
Than all the sages can.

∗34. Kenneth Slessor's "Five Bells"
Time that is moved by little fidget wheels
Is not my time, the flood that does not flow.
Between the double and the single bell
Of a ship's hour, between a round of bells

From the dark warship riding there below,
I have lived many lives, and this one life
Of Joe, long dead, who lives between five bells.

35. Eduardo Galeano's "Not Being the Master"
The wind whistles within me. I am naked. Master of nothing, master of no one, not even of my own convictions. I am my face in the wind, against the wind, and I am the wind that strikes my face.

36. Bishop Berkeley's "Tree"
If a tree falls in a forest and no one sees or hears it, does it really fall?

37. François Villon's "Where are the snows of yesteryear?" (*Où sont les neiges d'antan?*)

38. Joseph Heller's "Where are the Snowdens of yesteryear?"

39. Joseph Heller's *Catch-22*
There was only one catch and that was Catch-22. Orr would be crazy to fly more missions and sane if he didn't, but if he was sane he had to fly them. If he flew them he was crazy and didn't have to; but if he didn't want to he was sane and had to.

40. Enactment
I was walking with a student who was complaining loudly about how others were breaking the rules. We were both stopped by leopard slugs mating on the path in front of us.

I said: "Legislate this."

41. Jane Hirshfield's "Autobiography"

We do not end at our skin. To write about a tree with absolute objectivity is to write autobiography.

42 . Veronica's Moon (from Mark Edwards's "Late night conversations with a three-year-old")

Papa: Tell me Veronica, why is the moon so far away?
Veronica: It's not far away, Papa, it's just there in the night sky.

How do you respond?

43. Jack Kerouac's "Day and Night"

Day and night, why do they sojourn here?

*44. What Is Zen?

When my son was in his early teens he asked me, "What is Zen?"

"Well, it's like when you're out sailing and you are one with your yacht," I said.

"That sounds like when I'm having a good sail, Dad."

"And that's it too," I replied.

*45. Phillip McNamara's "How to Catch a Fish"

When I was young, my uncle would take me fishing along small creeks. The streams would mostly dry up in summer except for a couple of pools. I had many questions about the wonder of these pools.

I was told that these were unimaginably deep and that though divers had gone down to find out why the pools never dried up, the bottom had never been reached. I could see they were not wide enough for a submarine to explore. But I imagined that even a submarine would never reach the bottom.

My uncle said that the best fish lay in holes deep in those pools that never dried up. I was too scared to ever swim in them like he did, but I liked to imagine that one day I'd get a fishing line long enough to catch that fish.

*46. How do you find true freedom at work?

*47. Enlightenment is as enlightenment does.

*48. Dust on a Ruined Piano
Olivier Burckhardt: "What dust? . . . What mirror? . . . How can dust ever settle on a ruined piano?"

FOUR KOANS FROM THE BIBLE

49.
For now we see through a glass, darkly; but then face to face: now I know in part; but then shall I know even as also I am known. (1 Corinthians 13:12)

50. Judge not, that ye be not judged. (Matthew 7:1)

51.
Nor will people say, "Here it is," or "There it is," for behold the Kingdom of God is within you." (Luke 17:21)

52.

So we, *being* many, are one body in Christ, and every one members one of another. (Romans 12:5)

53. Was Christ Enlightened?

Nakagawa Soen Roshi was reading the Bible and encountered the passage, in Luke 23:43, where Jesus on the cross responds to the thief's entreaty: "Jesus, remember me when you come in your kingdom," with: "Truly I say to you, tonight you will be with me in paradise." Soen was despondent and said, "Jesus was not enlightened." He then searched out another account of the crucifixion, where Jesus responds to the thief: "Tonight you are with me in paradise." Soen said, "Thank goodness, Christ was enlightened."

54. Meister Eckhart's "The eye with which I see God is the eye by which God sees me."

55. How many angels can dance on the head of a pin?

TWO KOANS FROM SHAKESPEARE

56.
Men must endure
Their going hence even as their coming hither,
Ripeness is all.
—*King Lear,* Act 5 Scene 2

57.
My bounty is as boundless as the sea,
My love as deep; the more I give to thee,
The more I have, for both are infinite.
—*Romeo and Juliet,* Act 2 Scene 2

··᲻ ᲻··

58. Lewis Carroll's "Nobody"
"I see nobody on the road," said Alice.

"I only wish I had such eyes," the King remarked in a fretful tone. "To be able to see Nobody! And at that distance, too!"

59. Emily Dickinson's "In insecurity to lie is joy's insuring quality."

60. When you look in the mirror, who do you see?

61. Guo Gu's "Who is living this life?"

THREE KOANS FROM HASIDIC TRADITIONS

62. What Do You Pray With?

The Rabbi once asked his son: "What do you pray with?" The son understood the meaning of the question, namely on what he based his prayer. He answered, "With the verse, 'Every stature shall prostrate itself before thee.'" Then he asked his father, "And what do you pray with?" He said, "With the floor, the bench."

63. True Recognition

An old Rabbi asked his people, "How do you know when the night has ended and the day has begun?" After a while someone ventured, "Is that the moment when the individual trees begin to step out of the forest?" The old Rabbi shook his head, "No, it is not that moment." Another spoke up, "Is it the moment when you can tell a cloud from the morning mist?" "No," said the Rabbi, "it is not that moment." They all fell deeply silent and finally someone said, "Please tell us, Rabbi, how we can tell the moment when the night is ended and the day has begun?" And the Rabbi said, "It is the moment when you look into the face of a stranger and recognize your own."

64. Lighter

The Rabbi of Lublin once said: "How strange! People come to me weighed down from melancholy, and when they leave, their spirit is lighter, although I myself"—and here he was going to say "am melancholy," but he paused and then continued—"am dark and do not shine."

THREE DIALOGUES WITH MY DHARMA SUCCESSORS

65. Ian Sweetman's "Cutting Off All Conception"

I asked the Zen teacher Ian Sweetman, "What is the emptiness of emptiness?"

He responded, "The red flower in the vase."

*66. Mari Rhydwen's "Thank You"

Mari Rhydwen, Glenn Wallis, Arthur Wells, and I were giving an evening of short talks for students in Glenn Wallis's dojo in Dunedin after sesshin there. I gave one on gratitude, which was warmed by the fact that I had mislaid my wallet several times that day—and found it again. Each time I had it back in my hand I'd mumble, "Thank you, Universe." I continued, "I'm sure there must be a better way to express that." Mari chimed in, "Thank you."

67. Glenn Wallis's "Speak for Yourself"

At the time of Glenn Wallis's Dharma transmission in New Zealand, I was walking with Glenn and Arthur Wells, who are fellow teachers in New Zealand. I put my arms round both of their shoulders, and said, "Well done, you three." Glenn immediately responded, "Speak for yourself."

*68. John Gill's "Left Hand of God"

At the Federal Hotel, I heard John Gill play rags by Scott Joplin. During his break, I climbed up on the barstool beside him and asked him, admiringly, "How did you get to play like that?" He blew the head of his pint of dark brown Dogbolter, paused, then said, "You need the left hand of God."

69. Great Aunt Meditation

When the composer Michal Murin was driving me out from Bratislava to show me eastern Slovakia, he asked me a lot of questions about Zen and how to live it. I found his questions challenging—such questions always are—but they were more so because I spoke no Slovak, and he spoke just enough English for us to deal with practicalities.

When he asked me, "What is Zen?" I replied: "The countryside looks splendid now that the sun has come up." As always, after one of my responses, he remained silent. However, as we neared Lengow, his home village, he said: "I like the jokes in your religion, but I don't think I would do the meditation." Sensing my disappointment, he went on: "But I would do Great Aunt Meditation." "Well, what would that be?" I asked doubtfully. "Great Aunt Meditation is chicken meditation. My great aunt spends all afternoon in front of her fire. For hour after hour there she is in her chair, looking like she is asleep. But she knows where every chicken is, and which way the wind is blowing, and what loaf of rye bread the pantry mouse is munching."

In Lengow, I met Michal's great aunt. She was frail and almost totally blind. Michal talked family with her in Slovak. She responded in rivers of Ruthenian. I listened in English.

She plied me with Polish vodka. If you can't understand, at least you can drink!

Michal asked me to explain Zen to her. I said, "Ask her if the birds are singing in her heart!" Maybe he did, but she just poured me another vodka. As she labored to get another log on the fire, Michal told me that it took her an hour and a half to get to church. I asked how far it was, for the village was tiny. He replied that it was about a hundred meters. "Is it because she is blind, because she can barely walk?" "Yes. But mostly because she keeps stopping to enjoy what she can make out of the shadow and light. She picks up pebbles so she can feel them, talks to the dogs and cats, and to anyone she meets. It's a long journey."

70. Bird

When I finally got to meet Milan Adamciak, the father of experimental music in Slovakia, I was shocked to find that his arms were thinner than a child's and that his body was pitifully emaciated. A blonde beard, completely out of control, grew over his mouth. Yet after that first moment of recoil, I registered only his blue-green eyes, showing their pleasure as if a little breeze was blowing across a clear deep lake. He squeezed my left hand and said in uncertain English, "Good, good—doing something together." Under a West umbrella in central Bratislava we talked for five hours, chasing black coffee with black coffee, with never a beer. He told me many stories, but this is the one I remember best. "When I was twenty-one, I strapped my cello to my back and climbed a couple of thousand feet up onto a ridge in the high Tatras. It was just dawn. I unstrapped my cello, sat on a rock, and played my lowest C—soft and long. And the birds stopped their song—utterly. You could have heard a leaf move."

The hairs stand up in electrified attention along his arm.

"When I found the courage to play on at last, the birds shyly joined in, so that after a time, I couldn't say how long. I was a bird."

71. Sky and Ocean

Sky and ocean same gray;
nothing to tell me if I live or die.

72. Nonchoosing

A student asked me, "The poem 'Faith in Mind' says: 'The Great Way is not difficult, it just avoids picking and choosing.' How do you respond to that?"

"Now, I wonder—will I have a Vienna coffee or an espresso?" I replied.

"Not much trace of the lion's roar around here," said the student.

"Can I get you a latté, or will you settle for instant coffee?" I replied.

*73. Are You Enlightened?

Joko Beck had just finished a talk and asked if there were any questions. A young man raised his hand and bluntly asked, "Are you enlightened?" Her response was immediate. Laughing she said, "I hope I should never have such a thought."

74. Phillip McNamara's "Closer Than a Shadow"

My Australian Rules Football coach would often say to me, as a back-man whose job it was to prevent my opposition player getting hold of the ball, that I had to "follow him closer than his shadow." How would you follow closer than a shadow?

THE TIME BARRIER: SIX KOANS

*75. What is time?

*76. Nabokov's "Not Knowing Time"
"I wonder," said Ada, "I wonder if the attempt to discover those things is worth the stained glass. We can know the time, we can know a time. We can never know Time. Our senses are simply not meant to perceive it. It is like . . ."

*77. A Dilemma
We sense that our life has duration and is indeed the story of who we are. Yet for Joko Beck nothing has ever existed except this moment. As she put it: "That's all there is. That's all we are." How do you pass through the horns of this dilemma?

*78. Porchia's "Great Day"
My great day came and went, I do not know how. Because it did not pass through dawn when it came, nor through dusk when it went.

*79. Proust's "Freed from the Order of Time"
One minute freed from the order of time has recreated in us, in order to feel it, the person freed from the order of time. How do you manifest your own freedom from the order of time?

＊80. William Blake's "Eternity is in love with the productions of time."

81.
If we're watching TV together, and we both reach for the remote to change the channel at the same time, saying "terrible program"—is that one thought or two?

82. The Essence of Number
A student asked me, "The Dalai Lama says that all things are impermanent. What about numbers?"

I replied, "One, three, seven, eleven . . ."

"But those are all primes," she retorted.

"Sixteen, twenty-four . . ." I continued.

83. Mari Rhydwen's "Play the piano without using your hands."

84. W. B. Yeats's "How can we know the dancer from the dance?"

＊85. Gary Wallace's "Who Are Those Others?"
We spend so much time trying to get away from others, so as to avoid the pain of relationship. Only to find that the one that we have been trying to get away from is none other than our self. And then to realize that the only way to get away from self is to be with others.

What is the self?

86. Gary Snyder's "True Meditation"

Meditation is not just a rest from the turmoil of the stream of impurity in the world. It is a way of being the stream.

THREE KOANS ON THE THEME OF DEATH

*87. Who dies?

88. Arthur Wells's "What Does It Mean?"

Barry Magid, a Zen teacher in the lineage of Joko Beck, lost his wife Debbie in a plane crash. When people persist in asking, "What does Debbie's death mean?" he replies, "What is the meaning of the ocean? What is the meaning of the sky?"

What will your own death mean?

*89. Where do you go after you die?

··⊰ ⊱··

90. What Is Truth?

Gary Wallace asked: "What is truth?"

I responded, "You and I sitting here—the sun streaming through the window. How about for you?"

"I don't know," he responded. When I told Glenn Wallis about this, he said: "There you go."

*91. Joe Harding's "Good Morning"

Sitting early morning zazen by the mangroves of Port Pirie, the smoke of bushfires in the hills across the inlet drifting up towards the blue desert sky, already hot in a series of very hot days. My circumstances stranger than fiction and bleakly mirrored as I fill in days waiting for an alternator for my old bus that has the guys in the workshop scratching their heads and making calls to all kinds of places, including Japan where there's rumored to be one out there still, somewhere in the country.

I hear from out of the mangroves a man singing in a voice raspy with years of champion ruby smokes, but with flamboyant gusto "oh what a beautiful mornin', oh what a beautiful day, I've got a beautiful feeling everything's going my way." He does its ebullience justice, but doesn't follow it up with the other lines—he just leaves it hanging in the air, until a crow picks it up and flies off.

I hurriedly finish my zazen and turn to look for the source of this mysterious voice and expect to see the man, perhaps sitting behind me on a bench, but there is no one there. He is as invisible as the crickets that are already in high volume on this hot morning, and my cries of "hello, hello" draw the same response of emptiness, silence, before the chirping begins again. It is going to be another very hot day, so I get up and return to the motel room to wait for any news from the garage and watch the updates on the bushfires that are burning tenaciously all around us.

The next morning I again make my way to the mangroves to sit zazen, the heat has subsided and a fine drizzle of gray warm rain descends in gentle curtains across the smoldering landscape. It is the blessing that the people of Port Pirie have been praying for and I can almost hear the sizzle as fires in the distant hills begin to sputter and die.

I settle into sitting, and towards the end of my round

the man begins to sing those famous lines again "oh what a beautiful mornin', oh what a beautiful day, I've got a beautiful feeling everything's going my way." As with yesterday he is nowhere to be seen, the gray green mangroves keep him hidden and mysterious: he is there, but not there to be seen. I imagine him sitting there in his mangrove dojo, the warm rain beading in his tobacco-stained beard, a twinkle in his eyes.

I know better than to call out again, seeking an answer, and instead make my way back through the drizzle to the motel room to wait for any news from the garage and flick through the coverage of the fires, though this time the desperation to get going the way I always intended to has strangely left me.

What is the essence of true Dharma in Joe's story?

92. What would I be without my stories?

93. Glenn Wallis's "My words are not what I am saying."

94. Kathy Shiels's "Which Way Do You Look?"
At Christmas some in the west
Look to the star in the east
Which way do you look?

*95. Who is judging?

96. Can a robot meditate?

97. Contemporary Communication

Brigid's email from Bali: "I forgot to mention in my last email that on the way to the airport there was so much beautiful Geraldton Wax, one of my most beloved things about Perth."

Kathy's email from Perth: "Hugs and bunches of Geraldton Wax waving from the winds of winter."

Brigid's text on return: "Geraldton Wax extraordinarily radiant on the way home. Did you put it there?"

Kathy's text: "It's been in your eyes all the while my sweet!"

Brigid's text: "Yes! XXXX."

What is the essence of true Dharma in this exchange?

*98. Fionn's "The Finest Music in the World"

There is an old Irish story of the hero Fionn mac Cumhaill. Fionn asks his followers, "What is the finest music in the world?" They suggest answers: the cuckoo calling from the hedge, the ring of a spear on a shield, the song of the lark, the baying of a pack of hounds, the laughter of a gleeful girl, or the whisper of a beloved. "All good music," agrees Fionn. "But what is best?" they ask. Fionn answers: "The music of what happens is the finest music in the world."

What is the finest music in the world?

99. Stephen Crane's "March of the Mountains"

On the horizon the peaks assembled;
And as I looked,
The march of the mountains began.
As they marched, they sang,
"Aye! We come! We come!"

100. Phillip McNamara's "Stars in the Milky Way"

Whenever we went camping, we'd lay our swags out under the stars. The Australian sky is deep and endless but filled with the countless stars of the Milky Way. Amongst these we looked for and pointed out famous constellations. Tell me, how many stars are there in the Milky Way?

*101. Hume's "Piece of Coal"

When the philosopher David Hume was dying his friends gathered around him. James Boswell, Samuel Johnston's biographer, asked Hume: "David, what chance of an after-life?" Hume replied: "The same chance that that piece of coal won't ignite if you place it on the fire."

If you had been there, how would you have responded to Hume, beyond empirically testing his response?

*102. Koan on the Theme of Synchronicity

Synchronicities are like sparks from a great conflagration intimating the play of reality beneath and beyond our ordinary causal dualistic thinking.

What is that conflagration?

103. Save a rainforest.

TWO KOANS FROM ROBERT AITKEN'S
ZEN MASTER RAVEN

*104. Compassion

Mole spoke up after a long silence one evening and asked, "What's compassion?"

Raven said, "That's an inside story."

Mole asked, "Inside what?"

Raven said, "Stars on your fur."

105. The Spirit of Practice

Relaxing with others after zazen one evening, Owl asked,

"What is the spirit of the practice?"

Raven said, "Inquiry."

Owl cocked his head and asked, "What do I inquire about?"

Raven said, "Good start."

*106. Shakyamuni Realizes the Way

Robert Aitken said: "Shakyamuni Buddha looked up and saw the morning star, and exclaimed: 'I and all beings have at this moment attained the Way.' What did he realize?"

*107. Punctuality

Zen is precise about time, so much so that in the beginning years of practice, I thought that only those with good time management would get to experience eternity. When Robert Aitken came to Western Australia, I took him sightseeing. We were running late to pick up the senior student from Sydney, who was helping organize our first sesshin with a teacher. As we took in the view of the city, I asked him, "How do I show my family this splendor?"

"Be punctual," he replied.

What is the splendor?

*108. Aitken Roshi's "I'll Get Back to You"

I was in email dialogue with Robert Aitken. Our exchange concerned the concluding lines of Dongshan's poem "The Song of the Precious Mirror Samadhi":

Conceal your practice, function in secret,
seem for all the world like a fool or an idiot—
if you could only continue, it would be called
the host within the host.

In his translation, the last lines about the host within the host were missing. I asked him—it was irresistible—"So what is the host within the host, Roshi?"

"I'll get back to you on that," he emailed back.

Shortly after, I heard that he had died.

Where is Roshi now?

APPENDIX
Personal Accounts

Mari Rhydwen: Working on "Snow in a Silver Bowl"

Dr. Mari Rhydwen, who now more than twenty years on, is my co-teacher in the Zen Group of Western Australia, wrote me the following account of her experience of the synchronicities that occurred between the koan she was meditating on—"Snow in a silver bowl"—and a magnificent dream that she had at the time.

Koans and Synchronicity, by Mari Rhydwen

THIS IS a story of connections, of dreams, of talking. This is a story from the Tao.

Sometime in November 1994 I was talking with Ross on the telephone. At the time he was working on a musical piece based around the three daughter hexagrams of the I Ching. I told him how I had been reading about Zen in my mother's copy of the *Pears Encyclopedia*. In particular I told him about one section, which I quote below:

> The student must learn to act spontaneously without thinking, and without self-consciousness or hesitation. This is the main purpose of the koan, the logically insoluble riddle which the student must try to solve. One such is the question put by

master to pupil: "A girl is walking down the street,
is she the younger or the older sister?"

At this point, Ross asked me if I remembered my
response to Baoling's koan, "Snow in a silver bowl." I
could not recall it, but a few days later I looked it up
in my notes. I had written that I had told John Tarrant
Roshi that I was snow, that it was me and where I was
going, "No tracks."

"Is there any trace of you?" he asked.

"Yes," I replied, going on to tell him about my dream
which had culminated in my disappearing into snow,
the dream I call my Three Girls Dream. I did not tell
Roshi the whole of the dream in detail but I reproduce
it below.

The Three Girls Dream

Once upon a nighttime in a land faraway but ach-
ingly familiar, is a place where everybody meets.
It is inside a building, but it is outside too, public
space. It reminds me of Sydney's Queen Victoria
Building or the Strand Arcade and yet I know
that it is neither since, although I cannot see the
sky through the opaque skylights, I know from
the sepia tinge of the light, and the coldness, that
it is snowing outside. Many people are walking
around inside the building, but my attention is
focused on only four, three young women and
one man.

The women's attention is also focused on the

man, they are all in love with him. He is young
and good-looking with an animal energy that his
tight blue jeans do nothing to disguise. (A nice
shot here of crumpled blue-jean crotch!) The
women are all the same age but look strikingly
different. One is small, with straight short dark
hair, and she is pretty in a sharp, pinched kind of
way. She is always accompanied by her mother.
One is blond and soft. She is always smiling, calm
and confident. She has several younger siblings
whom she looks after tenderly as well as doing her
painting. The third girl has flowing red tresses and
pale skin. She wears white clothes that emphasize
her identification with pre-Raphaelite heroines.

It is this girl-woman, whom the young man
apparently loves, but we see them all wandering
separately around the building, passing on different levels, across landings, passing and passing.

The lovers meet secretly. She has to go outside the building to meet him down at the dock-
lands where he lives. She has to go down badly
lit alleyways and put up with the taunts of the
old men who live there, dirty old men who chew
tobacco and leer and make lewd comments when
she passes. She does not mind, she is wrapped in
the innocence of true love that she believes protects her.

One day the blond girl asks the young man if
he will pose for her. She has an art examination
the next day and must produce a life-drawing. He
agrees, she is flattered. He goes to her rooms in

the evening. They are suffused with candlelight, glowing and shadowy. The children, her little sisters and brothers, are there and they crowd into the bedroom where the young man is to pose. It is a beautiful scene, this young male, naked on a large high bed. The candlelight emphasizes the folds in the disheveled linen sheets, everything is golden, shadowy, heavy, and beautiful. Everyone is happy. It takes all night to make the drawings, capturing that mood, that dark-light, in charcoal and chalks.

The next morning the dark-haired girl meets the redhead and asks her if she knows where her lover spent the night. She then proceeds to inform her, omitting the information, which she knows, about the art exhibition and allowing the redhead to assume, as she is intended to, that her lover is having an affair with the blond.

The red-haired girl simply goes to the station and boards a white train. The dark-haired girl and her mother are there to see her off. The train sets off into the desert, pale stretches of sandy ground. Eventually the train stops. It is not exactly a station but it is a stopping place next to some habitation—it's where the blacks live. Here black men and women live in a kind of shantytown in the desert. They work all day, moving things around, collecting food, and they all work together, singing as they go. At night they sit around fires lit in old oil drums and tell stories. The girl stays with them. She works with them, she is happy and yet, she is not of them. She does not belong.

She gets on the train and continues her journey. Now the white train is moving into whiteness. There is no vegetation at all. Is it sand or snow? Where is the edge? Train and ground and sky are all one.

Back at the big building the dark dark-haired girl has revealed her treachery and so everyone knows the red red-haired girl is gone, gone for good. The young man is disturbingly unperturbed. The other two girls are distraught, especially the dark-haired one. All three of them realize that they never knew where the girl lived so they go together to see. It is downstairs, but inside the big building. It is a cell. Stone walls, and iron bed, one blanket. The only personal item is a small, blue, plastic Christmas tree. They all know this is the only present the young man ever gave her. It is all that remains of her. There is a feeling of such sadness.

Returning to the koan of snow in a silver bowl, via other sisters and more snow, I was able to delight in the way that working with koans is part of a vast dance. It dances itself in dreams and in telephone calls just as much as in the *dokusan* room. I am reminded of Wumen's Caution, "To treat each thought as realization is to trifle with your spirit." There is danger here. Yet, like discovering that the ubiquitous parking spaces that come with years of zazen are a shared secret, there is a sense of sangha involved when the dance I thought

I was dancing alone in the universe turns out to be choreographed to link an infinite cast across the boundary of dream and distance.

Ross Bolleter's Comment

There is so much beauty to lift the heart in Mari's dream, and the breathtaking correspondences between it and the koan of snow in a silver bowl. These range from her evocation of snow early on in the dream ("I know from the sepia tinge of the light, and the coldness, that it is snowing outside.") to the evocation of emptiness at the core of the dream: "Now the white train is moving into whiteness. There is no vegetation at all. Is it sand or snow? Where is the edge? Train and ground and sky are all one." At the same time, Mari's dream is so marvelously coherent as it fluently and seamlessly evokes love, art, pilgrimage, betrayal—and finally the most poignant sorrow.

Mari's concluding words—"the dance I thought was dancing alone in the universe turns out to be choreographed to link an infinite cast across the boundary of dream and distance"—catch us up, each and all, in the dance, and provide the deepest encouragement for us all to embark into the Way.

This dance, as it expresses itself through synchronicity, continues to the present day, interweaving past and future in an intimacy across time, which is to say that I found the copy of Mari's Three Girls Dream that she had given me in 1994 (along with its nest of correspondences to the koan "Snow in a silver bowl") in my chaotic study just as we were about to embark into a dialogue on the line, "A silver bowl filled with snow, the bright moon concealing egrets" from Dongshan's poem "The Song of the Precious Mirror of Samadhi," which represents the five ranks, metaphorically by means of the I Ching's three daughter hexagrams: *Li*, *Xun*, and *Dui*.

Surely, the deep sense of Mari's dream and its intimate association with the koan "Snow in a silver bowl" is that nothing occurs entirely of itself; rather everything is intimately related, and things happen in accord with the tendency of the whole to find its expression through our unique and particular circumstances.

Bob Joyner:
My Experience of Koan Work

I received from my student and successor Bob Joyner—now, and for the longest time, the teacher for the Adelaide Zen Group—the following account, which shows the changes wrought by koan study and realization on his life. These changes range across the three meanings of heart-mind: heart and its functions, mind and its functions, as well as, naturally, essence. Thus we are encouraged to realize and to live our realization in the midst of our activity.

Bob Joyner: My Account of Koan Work (1994)

LIKE MANY STUDENTS I commenced my koan work with Mu. The subsequent realization experience or kensho affected me in differing ways. Initially when I started Zen practice, I had the idea (like many others, I feel sure) that such an experience would solve most of my problems and that I would experience or undergo some kind of wonderful change. Well, it did—but not in the manner that I thought it would.

First, and most important to me at this stage, was that it proved to me in a practical sense that without doubt the Zen path was not just theory, just words. The teaching was true and now I could have faith in continuing my practice in it. This was important, for it sustained me over many years when only one sesshin a year was possible for me.

Second, as I've said, I thought it would solve many problems in my life—and in certain areas, such as the fear of death, it did. However (and there always seems to be a however), it seemed to create more problems than it solved. The experience of realization made me more open and along with continued zazen I felt myself more aware of the suffering around me together with such problems as increasing pollution and hostilities around the world. All this and more initially crowded in on me causing a great deal of confusion and anguish until I learned to deal with it at a personal level.

The third area growing out of all this was that of the experience of change. This was not immediate but gradually happened over the years as I continued koan work and zazen. Perhaps zazen may have been more the factor of change than koan work—but I do know both were involved. I suppose it could be said that the initial experience of self as other gradually deepened and carried into daily life and then affected me in numerous ways. For instance: my body posture and musculature became more flexible and supple which in turn influenced thought; I became more environmentally aware; I became gentler—my children stopped calling me "Oscar the Grouch"; in areas such as politics I voted for the common good rather than self-interest. And the list could go on.

With one or two exceptions individual koans did not have great impact on me. Rather, it was the ongoing koan path designed to deepen and widen that initial realization through making me personally see into each case upon my cushion and make it my experience that has had the effect. The stumbling through the "Koans after Kensho" deepening the experience from all angles into those covering the Buddha's teachings and then bringing these into daily life, into the marketplace, have had, I think, the intended effect.

Today, with still a way to go, I find myself integrating with much of what goes on around me. I love to travel on public transport, which provides glimpses of so many facets of my human nature. As trees and bushes in the garden, I shimmer in the wind. At the zendo and going to the deli I flow as traffic down the Great Eastern Highway. I live with a general acceptance of people and circumstance without judging. This doesn't happen perfectly or continuously or ideally—and may never—but that is why I continue with daily zazen and endeavor to push along with koan work as best I can. I guess that will always be the case.

Ross Bolleter's Comment

Bob's concluding paragraph shows how to live our realization, or more accurately, how our realization lives itself in our lives, as our lives. His words are an inspiration to us all to practice devotedly, to realize who we truly are, and to walk that realization into our lives, living it through the miracle of our everyday experience.

Phillip McNamara: Working with "Who Is Hearing That Sound"

"WHO IS HEARING that sound?" is a koan created by the fourteenth-century Japanese Zen master Bassui Tokushō (1327–1387). The koan as he proposed it was: "Who is the master of hearing that sound?" My purpose in writing this piece is to briefly indicate how working on "Who is hearing that sound?" provided me with equilibrium in a period where I could have lost my sanity and literally my hearing.

I was given the koan during a seven-day sesshin. Six months prior to attending the sesshin I had started to hear firework crescendo sounds in my left ear. These sounds would come and go. When they appeared, they were distracting and quite wearying. I initially tried to get rid of the sound by wriggling my ear with my finger, jutting my jaw back and forward, and tilting my head. I could feel fluid in my ear, and so I thought once that disappeared all would be right again. In the lead-up to sesshin these sounds had become quite regular, so when I was given the koan, I felt that it was an apt one to work with when I had almost constant weird sounds in my ear.

During sesshin the bells and clappers really set the firework sound going off permanently. Because we were meditating, I tried to only surreptitiously wriggle my ear, but by the middle of the sesshin that had stopped working as a remedy. The pitches and length of over-lapping individual sounds rang in a random fashion, but it basically sounded like the accelerating climax of a firework show happening in my left ear. As it didn't stop, I had to just allow the noise to sit, as I was, within the question of "Who is hearing that sound?"

After sesshin, the constant firework-like sounds did not stop. I am a high school teacher, and listening to students or colleagues through the sound was often difficult. Lying in bed at night, when the random nature of the popping and whizzing became very apparent, was equally as challenging. Meditating each morning and evening allowed the sounds to fill the whole world. I began to find them like bird song, the wind, wandering thoughts. They thus became the core sound for me when working on this koan. "Who is hearing it? Who?"

The symptoms also made me feel a bit bilious and dizzy. They made it difficult to distinguish some other sounds. During conversations I had to let the firework sounds pass straight through me or be distracted. During meditation I had to just sit and let it be. Walking kinhin, I was sometimes unsteady. These symptoms brought about the need for focused mindfulness, particularly when driving or writing, moving about, or carrying things. When not focused on the activity immediately at hand, I was focused on the koan. When the noise almost overwhelmed me, I would take a few moments to re-establish the question as the foundation of my experience: "Who is hearing that sound?"

Of course I went and had the phenomenon medically

checked. I went to several general practitioners and a range of medical specialists. My wife works in health care, and so I took her advice on who was regarded as the best specialists to see. I also checked on the Internet and read posts by people who had been afflicted with the same condition. Some had spontaneously healed, some had not, some were coping, and some were suicidal.

I had head and body scans, ear and heart tests. I saw a couple of ear, nose and throat specialists, a neurologist, a heart specialist, a vascular specialist, a psychologist, and my dentist. It cost a bit of money and a lot of time scheduling and traipsing around to the appointments. It was feared that it might be caused by something like multiple sclerosis or a tumor, so initial tests were to rule those out. They were. I continued on with my efforts to try to find a cause. I was given a number of theories but no cure. These included the advice that I needed a tooth removed (it was, but the sounds didn't stop); I was exaggerating the sounds and that they were a product of the stress of teaching; it was incurable tinnitus (I have tinnitus, but that is a mix of a high-pitched whistle and a low Gregorian chant and this new sound was quite loud and polyphonic); my ear was suddenly hearing the blood flow through the artery and draining from the veins behind it. I still thought it was fluid in my ear but each of the ENTs said it was not and refused to give me grommets to see if those cured it. To the contrary, one said that he had only seen one other case like mine and that the only cure was surgery to cut the vestibulocochlear nerve and make me permanently deaf in that ear. I refused. It would have also most likely made me bedridden.

Throughout all of this, a good eighteen months, I kept at my koan. Through the koan it became apparent that it is possible to transform what is negative into something positive, to change what appears unsupportive into something supportive.

My affliction was not visibly obvious to others; at times I just appeared clumsy or vaguely distracted. But for me it was constantly there and, according to a range of specialists, permanent. I accepted this and felt empathy with all those who carry on within the circumstances given to them. I developed a heightened sense of suffering for all beings and hence became somewhat more compassionate towards myself and all others; we all cope with what is given to us as best we can. I felt very sad for those on the Internet forum who had expressed their suicidal exasperation with the condition and hoped that they had started to ask themselves "Who is hearing that sound?"

The question had certainly kept me sane. Through it I had realized that there was no value to worrying about my noisy symptoms or conjecturing about where they might lead. The koan showed me that there was quite a distinction between the reality of the constant noise and my mind's experiencing of it. I realized that my thoughts, words, actions simply came out of the available internal and external stimulations. The koan showed me these were all reactions, mental exercises that I could either indulge in or let pass. I saw that thoughts often distort reality. I learnt that there is actually no need to activate, fuel, or feed thoughts and that at any stage of their arising we can let them go.

I began to see my condition as a state of grace.

I returned for the next seven-day sesshin, and during it moved on to other koans. The fireworks continued throughout, but I had accepted them and by then they were just another part of the landscape. Nevertheless on the drive home in conversation with another participant, I briefly explained my journey with sound. He felt sorry for me and casually said, "Perhaps having worked through the koan, your noises will now stop." A few kilometers down the road they abruptly did just that. The condition disappeared as quickly as it had arisen. A few years on the sounds have not returned. Without them each sound is now like a pebble dropping into water.

Bibliography

Aitken, Robert. *The Gateless Barrier: Wu-Men Kuan (Mumonkan)*. Translated with commentary by Robert Aitken. New York: North Point Press, 1991.

———. *The Mind of Clover: Essays in Zen Buddhist Ethics*. San Francisco: North Point Press, 1984.

———. *Zen Master Raven: The Teachings of a Wise Old Bird*. Boston: Wisdom Publications, 2017.

Beck, Charlotte Joko. *Nothing Special: Living Zen*. San Francisco: HarperOne, 1994.

Blackney, Raymond B. *Meister Eckhart: A Modern Translation*. New York: Harper & Bros, 1941.

Bolleter, Ross. *All the Iron Night*. Mt. Hawthorn, Western Australia: Smokebush Press, 2004.

———. *Dongshan's Five Ranks: Keys to Enlightenment*. Boston: Wisdom Publications, 2014.

———. *Du Piano-Épave / The Well Weathered Piano*. Nantes, France: Lenkalente Press, 2017.

———. *Piano Hill*. Fremantle, Australia: Fremantle Press, 2009.

Borges, Jorge Luis. *Labyrinths*. London: Penguin Books, 1970.

Burnet, James. *Early Greek Philosophy (3rd edition)*. London: A & C Black Ltd, 1920.

Caplow, Zenshin Florence, and Reigetsu Susan Moon eds., *The Hidden Lamp: Stories from Twenty-Five Centuries of Awakened Women*. Boston: Wisdom Publications, 2013.

Carroll, Lewis. *Alice's Adventures in Wonderland & Other Stories*. New York: Barnes & Noble, Inc., 2010.

Chang Chung-Yuan. *Original Teachings of Ch'an Buddhism*. New York: Vintage Books, 1971.

Ende, Michael. *Momo*. Translated by J. Maxwell Brownjohn. London: Puffin, 1984.

Fields, Rick. *How the Swans Came to the Lake: A Narrative History of Buddhism in America*. Boston: Shambhala Publications, 1992.

Fitzgerald, F. Scott. *The Great Gatsby*. New York: Scribners, 1925.

Ford, James Ishmael. *Zen Master Who? A Guide to the People and Stories of Zen*. Boston: Wisdom Publications, 2006.

Galeano, Eduardo. *The Book of Embraces*. Translated by Cedric Belfrage. New York: W. W. Norton & Co. Inc, 1992.

Gammage, Bill. *The Biggest Estate on Earth: How Aborigines Made Australia*. Sydney: Allen & Unwin, 2011.

Gleick, James. *Time Travel: A History*. London: 4th Estate, 2016.

Guardini, Romano. *Rilke's "Duino Elegies": An Interpretation*. Translated by K. G. Knight. Washington, DC: Henry Regnery, 1961.

Larkin, Philip. *Collected Poems*. London: Faber & Faber, 2004.

Lawrie, Margaret, ed. *Myths and Legends of Torres Strait*. St. Lucia, Queensland, Australia: University of Queensland Press, 1970.

Levine, Stephen and Ondrea. *Who Dies?* New York: Anchor Books, 1982.

Loori, John Daido, ed. *Sitting with Koans: Essential*

Writings on Zen Koan Introspection. Boston: Wisdom Publications, 2006.

Miura, Isshu, and Ruth Fuller Sasaki. *Zen Dust: The History of the Koan and Koan Study in Rinzai (Linji) Zen*. Melbourne and Basel: Quirin Press, 2015.

Nabokov, Vladimir. *Ada or Ardor: A Family Chronicle*. New York: McGraw Hill, 1969.

Neruda, Pablo. *Selected Poems*. Translated by Nathaniel Tarn and Anthony Kerrigan. Boston: Houghton Mifflin Harcourt, 1990.

Priestley, J. B. *Man and Time*. Garden City, NY: W H Allen, 1964.

Proust, Marcel. *A la recherche du temps perdu*. Translated by C. K. Scott Moncrieff as *Remembrance of Things Past*. New York: Random House, 1981.

Proust, Marcel. *A la recherche du temps perdu*. Volume 6. Translated by Ian Patterson as *Finding Time Again* (New York: Penguin, 2003).

Rilke, Rainer Maria. *The Selected Poetry of Rainer Maria Rilke*. Translated by Stephen Mitchell. New York: Vintage Books, 1984.

Slessor, Kenneth. *Selected Poems*. New York: HarperCollins, 1993.

Tanahashi, Kazuaki. *Moon in a Dewdrop: Writings of Zen Master Dogen*. New York: North Point Press, 1985.

Tarrant, John. *Bring Me the Rhinoceros and Other Koans That Will Bring You Joy*. Boston: Shambhala Publications, 2008.

Wenger, Michael. *Forty-Nine Fingers*. San Francisco: Dragons Leap Press, 2011.

Yamada, Koun. *Zen: The Authentic Gate*. Boston: Wisdom Publications, 2015.

Credits

I am grateful to the following teachers, students and friends who created, unearthed, or enacted various koans within the sequence of 108 koans that constitutes part 3 of this book: Robert Aitken: 104–8; John Tarrant: 6, 20, 53, 80; Susan Murphy: 18, 40, 43, 56, 62, 63; Mari Rhydwen: 66, 83; Ian Sweetman: 65; Glenn Wallis: 15, 67, 78, 93; Arthur Wells: 7, 86, 88, 103; Nick Arnold: 12; Britta Biedermann: 8; Chris Barker: 21; Olivier Burckhardt: 48; Tony Coote: 2; Richard Davis: 19; Paul Doughty 99; Lizabeth Finn: 39; Joe Harding: 91; Brigid Lowry: 97; Phillip McNamara: 45, 74, 100; Judith Peppard 29; Kathy Shiels 60, 94, 97, 98; Jane Taylor: 22; Gary Wallace: 85, 90.

Index

About the Author

ROSS BOLLETER is the author of *Dongshan's Five Ranks*, and is a Zen teacher in the Diamond Sangha tradition. He trained with Robert Aitken and John Tarrant and received Transmission from them in 1997. He is also a composer with numerous album releases, especially in the field of ruined piano. His book of poems, *Piano Hill*, was published by Fremantle Press in 2009. He teaches in Australia and New Zealand and has successors in both places. Ross has two grown-up children, Amanda and Julian, and is a grandfather twice over.

What to Read Next
from Wisdom Publications

INTRODUCTION TO ZEN KOANS
Learning the Language of Dragons
James Ishmael Ford

"This much-needed book will invite, challenge, and inspire you."—Ross Bolleter

ENTANGLING VINES
A Classic Collection of Zen Koans
Thomas Yuhō Kirchner
Foreword by Nelson Foster

"A masterpiece. It will be our inspiration for 10,000 years."—Robert Aitken, author of *Taking the Path of Zen*

SITTING WITH KOANS
Essential Writings on Zen Koan Introspection
John Daido Loori and Thomas Yuhō Kirchner

"Required reading for those interested in how koans are used in Zen practice."—*Shambhala Sun*

About Wisdom Publications

Wisdom Publications is the leading publisher of classic and contemporary Buddhist books and practical works on mindfulness. To learn more about us or to explore our other books, please visit our website at wisdompubs.org or contact us at the address below.

Wisdom Publications
199 Elm Street
Somerville, MA 02144 USA

We are a 501(c)(3) organization, and donations in support of our mission are tax deductible.

Wisdom Publications is affiliated with the Foundation for the Preservation of the Mahayana Tradition (FPMT).